T0196168

Heaven in the Orchard

Hints of the Divine in Daily Life

TED AUBLE

iUniverse, Inc.
Bloomington

Heaven in the Orchard
Hints of the Divine in Daily Life

Copyright © 2012 Ted Auble

iUniverse books may be ordered through booksellers or by contacting:

iUniverse
1663 Liberty Drive
Bloomington, IN 47403
www.iuniverse.com
1-800-Authors (1-800-288-4677)

ISBN: 978-1-4759-5701-3 (sc)
ISBN: 978-1-4759-5702-0 (e)

Library of Congress Control Number: 2012919529

Printed in the United States of America

iUniverse rev. date: 10/24/2012

Introduction

In *Heaven in the Orchard*, Father Ted Auble shares reflections drawn from a wealth of personal experiences as a theology student at the Catholic University of Louvain, Belgium, as a Peace Corps volunteer in South Korea, and as a priest ordained to minister in the diocese of Rochester, New York, in 1975.

Each one of the brief selections in *Heaven in the Orchard* is intended to be read as a single, standalone piece. Many have found this format employed in Father Auble's previous book, *Divine Sparks: Gospel Stories Discovered in Everyday Life*, both helpful for their own personal reflections and easy to use. The Bible references at the head of each section represent the scriptural relationship to the text that follows.

All Biblical quotations found in *Heaven in the Orchard* are taken from *The New American Bible* and are used with permission.

The Orchard

Unless a grain of wheat falls on the ground and dies, it remains only
a single grain of wheat, but if it dies, it yields a rich harvest.
—John 12:24

Imagine for a moment you are holding an apple seed in the palm of your hand. Most of us don't normally think much about these minor nuisances found at the core of the apple. We just throw them away and carry on. But take a moment to look at this tiny potential for life.

Now imagine you are standing in the middle of an apple orchard on a warm, sunny, mid-May morning with just the slightest hint of a breeze in the air. The air itself is filled with subtle sweetness, and there is a constant buzzing all around. As you look up and down the rows of trees and see the soft clouds of the most delicate pink all around, it is clear the orchard is in full bloom. The bees are feverishly working, visiting every blossom to drink in its sweetness. The orchard is teeming with life.

Next imagine it is two months later. July has come to the orchard, and the sun is very hot. There is no sign of the soft pink blossoms of May. Now you see green, lush, leathery foliage everywhere. While it is hot in the sun, the leaves provide a cool resting place and invite you to lie down beneath their shade. As you look up through the branches of each tree, you discover small clusters of round green apples slowly growing, swelling day by day. The life in the orchard continues to expand ever so gradually even while you lie back to enjoy a lazy summer nap.

Soon autumn arrives at the orchard. There is a crispness to the air that invigorates, makes you feel alive and energized. The trees again have changed in their character. They are bent over now under the burden of their fruit. Everywhere you look the branches are laden with clusters of deep red or golden orbs. The time has come, and the orchard is ready.

The harvesters arrive with trucks, ladders, cars, crates, and baskets. Soon the entire scene is pulsating with lively activity. Workers fill the air with chatter and laughter. Occasionally someone bites into the firm, juicy flesh of an apple—crunch! So sweet. Yet it is only the foretaste of what lies ahead: pies, pastries, applesauce, cider, juice, and more.

Try to imagine for a moment that you never saw an apple or an apple tree or an orchard. All you have ever seen is this tiny seed in your hand. Would you, in your wildest imagination, be able to envision the life it is capable of yielding?

That is what Jesus was getting at when he mentioned the seed falling to the ground. Looking at an apple seed and trying to imagine the life of the orchard and the fruit it produces without ever having seen an apple is like looking at our life here on Earth and trying to imagine what the resurrection, what heaven, is really like. Our life here can seem so rich and vibrant. And it is, but it is only the tiny hard-coated shell of the life that awaits us in resurrection, a dynamic fullness beyond all expectations.

The stories and reflections that follow are meant to be "seeds" for your thoughts and experiences. Each short selection is an invitation to examine the seeds of your own experiences, as ordinary as they may seem, and to discover the rich life that lies hidden beneath the surface. May your stories lead you to discover *Heaven in the Orchard*.

Hunger

Deuteronomy 26:4–10; Romans 10:8–13; Luke 4:1–13

It must have been my fourth birthday, possibly my fifth. All the grandparents had gathered at our house for a big Sunday dinner and birthday celebration. My grandmas were out in the kitchen helping Mom, who was busy preparing a complete turkey dinner with all the trimmings. The delicious, seductive aromas wafted from the kitchen, filling the house, while the men of the family sat telling stories in the living room. I can still hear my grandfather telling yet another one of his stories of the hunt while everyone listened attentively. The dining room sat quietly awaiting the crowd. The table was resplendent with the special cloth and dishes that made their appearance only for special occasions. And in the center of the table sat my birthday cake, all decorated with roses made of colorful frosting.

And I was hungry. Very hungry. I can still smell the turkey roasting, still see the bustle in the kitchen as I entered that adult world to voice my need. "I'm hungry."

Mom was so busy orchestrating and coordinating dinner that my little voice must have seemed a minor distraction as she answered somewhat absently, "We'll be having dinner in an hour."

An hour! When you're four years old, an hour might as well be a week! I was hungry *now*! So, satisfied that I had presented my need through the proper channels, yet still hungry because my request had fallen on deaf, or at least distracted, ears, I decided to take matters into my own hands. I went back into the dining room and looked at that beautiful cake. There it was, sweet, colorful, tempting—and available. No, it wasn't just available. It virtually cried out to me. It was my birthday cake, after all. So I climbed onto a chair, reached out over the table, and with my tiny fingers very carefully ate all the roses off the cake.

Have you ever been desperately hungry? Just after his baptism Luke tells us that Jesus went into the desert, which in Scripture can be both a place of testing and of meeting God. Once there, Jesus ate nothing for forty days. In

3

typical Lucan understatement, he says afterward, Jesus "was hungry" (Luke 4:2). He must have been desperately, ravenously hungry.

So Satan, the tempter arrives. "If you are the Son of God—and at your baptism we all heard the voice from heaven say you are—then make this stone into bread." The suggestion seems reasonable enough, maybe even innocent. What harm? Why not? After all, one has to eat something to keep body and soul together. Besides, there is no supermarket nearby, no handy source of food. The problem, which Jesus recognized at once, is that this marks the first step down a slippery slope. First satisfy your need for comfort, then power, and then attention. It's all about you.

To further complicate matters, in fact it *is* all about Jesus, but not in an egotistical, self-serving way. That is where these tests lead. And it is definitely not who Jesus is. The truth of these tests, which Jesus unmasks one by one, is that they all attempt to draw him away from the mission of his humanity, a humanity he assumed at his birth, a humanity in which he was immersed in the waters of his baptism in the Jordan, a humanity he carried into the desert.

In his humanity, Jesus knew hunger just like we do, not just physical hunger but all the hungers of the human soul, all the longing for fulfillment and wholeness. As human beings our hungers serve a purpose. They signal what we need to survive. But they do more than that. They serve to show us we are finite, we are dependent, we are mortal. Our hungers prompt us to look beyond the distractions of daily life to the profound mystery that gave us life in the first place, sustains our lives now, and breathes in us with every breath. That ever-present divine mystery will be there to embrace us even as we breathe our last breath. Our hungers teach us what it means to be human, to be dependent on God, and to be interdependent on one another.

My! How You've Changed

Nehemiah 8:2–6, 8–10; 1 Corinthians 12:12–30; Luke 1:1–4, 4:14–21

Not long ago I attended a meeting in what had once been the convent at the parish school where I grew up. The building itself brought back so many memories from childhood. I remember the Franciscan sisters in their brown habits with the enormous rosaries hanging from the white cords with the three knots in them tied around their waists, the knots reminders of their vows of poverty, chastity, and obedience. I remembered being a student in their classes, always a bit intimidated if not downright fearful of them, yet at the same time awestruck by their apparent spirituality. The convent where they lived was the inner sanctum, closely guarded and as off limits as the Holy of Holies of the ancient temple. No one ever got beyond the side door. Once I remember taking a basket of apples to the sisters with my mom. We were allowed to go as far as the kitchen. I felt truly privileged to be standing on such holy ground.

But those days are long past, and the sisters no longer live there. So when I had the chance to tour the rest of the building, I couldn't resist. How tiny their rooms were and how confining their lives must have been. My respect for them only grew. It had to take an enormous dedication to live the life these sisters led.

After the meeting was over and I had taken my little tour, I found I still had a little extra time and decided to walk the same path—between my old school and the home where I had grown up—that I had traveled for nine years as a youngster. As I strolled along the same route I had taken for all those years, the memories came flooding back. So many things were just where I remembered them, but so many looked so different.

I passed the street where my best friend used to live and recalled all the great times we'd had creating miniature golf courses in his backyard, doing homework together, and just hanging out together. I saw the public school I passed every day wondering what it must be like to be a student there. It always seemed intimidating to me. I passed the yard that used to have a lovely garden all along the path. I remembered every September that garden was

5

filled with fragrant marigolds and cosmos. Now it was gone. There are only overgrown weeds and trees no one ever planted growing there.

I was surprised at how the distance between home and school had somehow been shortened and the fact that it was no longer uphill each way. In my old neighborhood I found all the houses had moved closer together and the yards were much smaller.

As I walked down the street I remembered the names, faces, and families who used to live in each of the houses. Mrs. Shapiro lived across the street and used to bring us kids hard candy whenever she went shopping downtown. Down the street a few houses Mr. Schipper had a huge vegetable and fruit garden in the extra lot next to his house. That's all gone now. There is a house there. As I remembered the old neighbors, I realized they too were all gone now and I was a total stranger there.

That was when reality hit me. Not only had the old neighborhood changed, I had changed as well. It is true that you can never really go back home, a truth Jesus experienced too.

When he returned to Galilee "in the power of the spirit," he had changed dramatically. He had been baptized by John the Baptist, seen the Spirit descend upon him, and heard the Father's voice from heaven proclaim him to be the beloved Son. He had fasted in the desert for forty days and nights and engaged in a threefold battle with Satan. He had begun teaching throughout the region of Galilee and even curing some sick people. A lot had happened in his life since he'd left home. So when he arrived in Nazareth amid much buzz, Jesus was no longer just the son of the neighbors Mary and Joseph, the carpenter.

Just how profoundly Jesus had changed soon became evident as Jesus entered the synagogue on the Sabbath, as all devout Jews did, took the scroll of the prophet Isaiah, found the passage that read, "The spirit of the Lord is upon me because he has anointed me" and then sat down and said, "Today this Scripture passage is fulfilled in your hearing" (Luke 4:21). Thus he delivered one of the shortest homilies ever given.

The power of his few words was explosive. We can see just how explosive if we read a little further and hear the reaction of his listeners. By claiming to fulfill this Scripture passage Jesus claimed to be anointed, in Hebrew,

Messiah; in Greek, *Christ*. Along with this shocking claim came the signs of the anointed of God:

- *Glad tidings to the poor.* This is the beginning of the age of inclusion. The poor are not just those without earthly possessions; they are all those people the rest of society overlooks, tucks away out of sight, or just plain rejects.
- *Liberty to captives.* This implies not only physical freedom but forgiveness of debts, even forgiveness of sins. It means the repair and restoration of broken relationships, especially with God.
- *Recovery of sight to the blind.* Again, not just physical sight, although Jesus did heal a number of blind persons, but another level of sight: insight into what matters in life. A good example of that is found in the account of Ezra, the scribe reading the law to the crowds in the book of Nehemiah (Nehemiah 8:2–10). The crowd that gathered to hear the sacred books read were newly returned exiles from Babylon. They may have, in large part, lost touch with their traditions. They may have even lost touch with a sense of meaning and direction in life. That may well be the reason they wept when they heard their own sacred texts read and discovered a God who cared for them and was present to them all along. Where had they been? In a similar fashion Jesus opened eyes to see God intimately present and involved with each human life.

But where does all this leave us? Jesus said, "Today this Scripture passage is fulfilled in your hearing." When we were anointed at baptism, we were changed and now share in the mission of the Anointed One, the Christ. It falls to us now to see that good news is proclaimed to the poor.

- Who are the poor today?
- Who is overlooked or shunned in our culture today? How can we include them?
- Who can we set free simply by forgiving? Might we actually set ourselves free by forgiving others? Who can we set free by affirming their personal worth and dignity?
- How can we restore sight to the blind?
- How do our actions reveal the presence of the Spirit within?

"Realizing" the Kingdom

Isaiah 8:23–9:3; 1 Corinthians 1:10–13, 17; Matthew 4:12–23
I believe that unarmed truth and unconditional
love will have the final word in reality.
—Dr. Martin Luther King Jr. accepting the Nobel Peace Prize

It was messages like this delivered with great passion and conviction that drew people to listen almost spellbound to this mid-twentieth-century American. His words inspired. Wherever he went, the crowds gathered. As time went on the crowds continued to grow. What was it about him? What was the attraction? Some would say he offered hope. Some would say he offered a new direction, a new perspective, or a new path. Still others would say he spoke to the deepest yearnings of the human heart.

One could suggest that it was for the very same reasons that people followed Jesus of Nazareth two thousand years earlier. With just a casual reading of Matthew's gospel story of how Jesus called his first disciples, it would seem that it was the sheer force of his compelling presence that drew people to him. One might get the impression that Jesus just happened to be walking along the shore one day, saw these fishermen, called them to follow, they looked at each other and said, "That's a good idea," and immediately dropped everything to follow this mysterious, charismatic, itinerant preacher. Certainly Jesus was a charismatic person and his presence was undoubtedly compelling, but would these seasoned fishermen really be inclined to follow a complete stranger? It is possible. But if we carefully examine the story just as Matthew tells it, the characters take on more depth. Their humanity shows through, and their actions flow more naturally.

Matthew tells us that Jesus had moved from Nazareth after the death of John the Baptist and went to live in Capernaum on the Sea of Galilee. Jesus actually set up housekeeping there and began preaching and announcing the nearness of the kingdom of heaven. Now it is reasonable to assume that in a small town like Capernaum, word would get around quickly, especially when there was a new and inspiring teacher in town. Naturally, people would want to come and hear him themselves and see what they thought of him. And it is also reasonable to assume that Simon and his brother, Andrew, as well as James and John would have been among those who went to hear this new teacher.

Jesus's message was "Repent, for the kingdom of heaven is at hand"—in other words, "Change the direction in which you are looking for happiness. God is already here in your life. You only need to look." The evidence he presented and the truth he spoke—forgiveness, acceptance, and unconditional love—resonated in the hearts of his listeners. It is, after all, what the human heart longs for. This encounter was only the beginning, the groundwork for the mission to come. The excitement generated by this stranger may well have prompted people to ask themselves whether the kingdom of heaven could actually be dawning.

One could imagine Peter and company hearing that message and then returning to their boats to reflect on what Jesus offered as they washed and repaired their nets. They might even have talked about him and asked each other's opinion of him as they went about their daily chores.

The stage was set. The time was right. It was then that Jesus decided to take a walk along the shore. He might well have recognized Simon and Andrew as faces he had seen in the crowd listening to him. They certainly knew who he was. One can imagine that when Jesus called these first disciples, the tiny spark of expectation that had been kindled in their hearts burst into the full-blown flame of hope. They dropped everything, followed him, and never looked back. The invitation was too enticing to pass up. The kingdom Jesus announced was the fullness of God's rule on Earth, acknowledged by all creation. They had high hopes. And those hopes were only validated further as they accompanied Jesus around Galilee. They listened to him preach and witnessed him heal all manner of disease and illness. What these first disciples saw was evidence that the kingdom really was dawning among them. It was all very inspiring, very exciting.

So what happened? Here we are two thousand years later and the kingdom does not seem to have dawned any further. If anything, one could argue that it seems to have disappeared altogether. There is so much darkness in our world. But the gospel message today is the same as it was two thousand years ago.

The kingdom continues to dawn among us today even if it has still not yet fully arrived. God is still here in our lives. We need only look.

There may be many ways we are cared for and cared about, prayed for and prayed about that we do not even know. And then there are the people in our lives we tend to take for granted or even overlook because they are always there for us. It's almost as if they were invisible—not because they don't mean anything to us but because they are so much a part of our lives, like a breath or a heartbeat. All of these are evidence of God's care and presence in our lives. All of these are evidence of the kingdom of heaven among us.

But there's more. In the Catholic tradition, whenever we gather to celebrate the Eucharist we are often reminded that the kingdom is still dawning among us. At the offertory, as the bread and wine are brought forward through the assembly, I like to think there is another "hidden collection" taking place. As the paten bearing the hosts to be consecrated at the altar moves through the assembly, every life it passes is piled on so that when it finally reaches the altar the life of every person present is on that paten and is offered to God. Everything we have done during the week. Every triumph, every failure, every gift given and every gift refused, every fault and every virtue is offered to God. All of it—the good, the bad, and the ugly. It is a profound reminder that God takes our lives just as they are, accepts us just as we are, and transforms us with his own life. Truly, the kingdom of heaven is at hand, but not entirely. At least, not yet.

Again, we are reminded that the kingdom is a work in progress at the time we pray the Lord's Prayer. We remember that we are totally dependent on God and that the kingdom is God's work in God's good time, but that we have a role to play in the building up of the kingdom. We need to have the humility to admit that sometimes we hurt one another and that we need to be forgiving as well as forgiven. Reflecting on the word proclaimed at the Eucharist, offering our lives to God and recognizing our poverty all serve to help us prepare to build the kingdom of heaven.

The more closely we follow Jesus, the more faithfully we live as he lived the more evident the kingdom becomes and the brighter the light shining in the darkness—and there is plenty of darkness out there still. But that should not intimidate or discourage us. At the beginning of John's gospel we are told that the light shined in the darkness and the darkness could not overcome it. Not even on Good Friday, when the darkness threw everything it had against the light. For there is always the radiant, brilliant, and triumphant light of Easter Sunday when life rose from the grave and death itself was vanquished. That is the final word.

Fire!

Zephaniah 2:3, 3:12–13; 1 Corinthians 1:26–31; Matthew 5:1–12

The forest just outside Clairvaux, Luxembourg, had caught on fire. I watched columns of gray smoke mix with huge orange flames in the summer sky as crews battled to get it under control. And it was a battle. As the fire raged it superheated the surrounding trees, which then suddenly exploded into flames from top to bottom, completely consuming them. Then their neighbors would repeat the violent cycle and the forest quickly became a roaring inferno spreading faster and faster as the flames themselves became hotter and hotter, even creating their own wind, further fanning the flames.

Meanwhile, the firefighters used every technique they had to battle this growing monster, including water, of course, but also back-burning and hacking away at vegetation in the fire's path to create a firewall that would deprive the fire of fuel. It was the only way to stop this runaway destruction.

When Jesus went up the mountain, sat down, and began to teach the crowd gathered around, he gave them the tools for building a firewall—not against forest fires but against the much more insidious, stubborn, and self-perpetuating destructive forces of hatred, violence, greed, selfishness, and alienation.

Imagine what our world would be like if every human being on Earth lived these simple yet challenging beatitudes. It would stop dead in its tracks the raging inferno of war, genocide, violence of every kind. It would put an end to hostility, resentment, and fighting—right down to the petty squabbles children have over computer time or whose turn it is to do the dishes. It would create a world of justice, compassion, understanding, and, yes, at last, peace. On the surface the beatitudes appear to be so simple. They *are* simple, just not easy.

The eight beatitudes require us to take away the fuel that feeds all this destruction in our world. To do that you might say they require us to become "shock absorbers," in a sense. That means not returning hurt for hurt or evil for evil when that is what we are *so tempted* to do. That does not mean that being a shock absorber is the same as being a doormat. I doubt anyone would consider Jesus, Mohandas Gandhi, or His Holiness, the Dalai Lama, doormats.

What the beatitudes do is offer us a way to take the hurt and pain we receive and transform it internally by the vision they offer, a vision of who we are and what we are capable of becoming. For example:

- If we *hunger and thirst for righteousness,* then we look for right relationships with God, others, and creation.
- If we *are pure of heart,* what we say and what we do agree. It's called integrity.
- If we *are peacemakers,* we know all true peace comes from God. In our community, that peace has rested on the bedrock of *forgiveness* since Easter afternoon.

But forgiveness is such a misunderstood word I want to briefly say what forgiveness is *not:*

- Forgiveness does not mean what you did is okay. It isn't.
- Forgiveness does not mean I understand. I don't.
- Forgiveness does not mean I am not angry. I may be angry for a long time and passionately wish that what you did had not ever happened.
- Forgiveness does not mean I am not hurt. I may be very hurt for a long time. It may even be a wound that will never entirely heal.
- Forgiveness does not mean I will forget. This is my favorite. Where in the world did we get the notion that forgiveness requires forgetting? So often I hear people say, "I know, I know. I'm supposed to forgive and forget." Where does this come from? I cannot find anywhere in the gospels where Jesus instructs us to forget. He does repeatedly call us to forgive, but forgetting? In fact, there is strong evidence that he himself did not forget Peter's threefold denial. After his resurrection Jesus gave Peter the chance to cancel out his denials with a threefold confession of love (John 21:15–17). What we need to do is forgive. Let forgetting take care of itself.
- Forgiveness does not necessarily mean reconciliation. It may lead to that and if it does it is a grace-filled moment. But sometimes there are certain

people who simply should not be together. Abusive relationships come to mind as an example.

So if forgiveness is not any of these things, what is it? Forgiveness boils down to this: the willingness to live with an uneven score. It means I give up the desire and the attitude that I have a right to get even, to pay back (usually with interest, if we are honest).

Forgiveness acts as a shock absorber. It's very simple, just not easy. This might help. Maybe when we find it difficult to be a shock absorber we might pray simply,

"Holy Spirit, help me to hold what I cannot now heal." If we do not transform our pain, we will transmit it. Then we would just be like another tree in the raging forest fire, bursting into flame and spreading the hurt even further. But with the help of the Holy Spirit and the vision of the beatitudes, we can build a firewall and turn evil into good and hurt into healing.

What's in a Name?

Exodus 3:1–8, 13–15; 1 Corinthians 10:1–6, 10–12; Luke 13:1–9

Up until the very first day of kindergarten, I knew my name was Teddy. But that first day of school brought more than the average trauma for this five-year-old when the teacher called me "Theodore." I was confused. I thought she was talking to someone else! At home later that day the mystery was solved when Mom explained "Teddy" was short for Theodore and that she named me that because she always wanted a son named Teddy. And so I resigned myself to the fact that for the next nine years I would be known as "Theodore." Only many years later did I begin to appreciate—and, I admit—even enjoy the fact that Theodore comes from two Greek words meaning "gift of God." That little tidbit used to make my father roll his eyes whenever I pointed it out. And it got better. With a little research I found out that my patron, St. Theodore, was a Christian soldier so filled with zeal he went around burning down pagan temples. Looking around at all my friends I discovered nearly everybody else had a patron saint who was an angel, an apostle, a virgin, a martyr, or even a king or queen. I got an arsonist.

How did you get your name? Were you named after a parent, grandparent, family hero, or favorite saint? Names are important. They are part of us, who we are, our identity. Jesus got his name from an angel who told Joseph the baby to be born was to be named "Jesus, because he will save his people from their sins" (Matthew 1:21).

But what is God's name? There is of course the familiar story about the first grader who knew that answer. He pronounced with great confidence, "God's name is Andy."

"Andy?" the teacher asked.

"Yup, Andy," he replied, "because we sing in church about walking in the garden with him: 'Andy walks with me. Andy talks with me. Andy tells me I am his own.'"

Moses, however, received a much more profound and mysterious response to that question when God spoke from a burning bush that was not consumed by the flames and said, "I am who am." The name is written in four Hebrew letters and is considered so sacred it is never pronounced out loud. For hundreds of years Scripture scholars and theologians along with all the rest of us have wondered what in the world it means. "I am who am" can mean so many different yet related things—among them: God cannot *not* be. God is utterly transcendent, mysterious, infinite, eternal, unknowable; yet at the same time God is totally imminent, present in every particle of the universe, in the every fiber of your being, in your heart and soul.

When I was studying theology one of my professors asked me on my final exam, "How can God be totally transcendent and totally imminent at the same time? Aren't the two mutually exclusive?" At the time I really struggled with my response, but now I have reached the conclusion that God is definitely transcendent and unknowable just as the universe is unknowable. We can know part of it, but we will never be able to fully grasp the entire vastness of the universe. On the other hand, we can look up at the night sky, spellbound at its beauty and majesty. We can delight in picking out various constellations and planets and know part of the universe. Every once in a while we have encounters with the unknowable God, sometimes at the most unexpected times and in the most ordinary of circumstances—a smile or a tear, a kind word, or even in silence.

Because this God is so present, God heard and felt the suffering of the Israelites in their slavery in Egypt. This God is compassionate because this God has suffered with the people. And compassion makes this God unlike any other god—a point Jesus emphasizes when questioned by people struggling to understand why God punished those poor Galileans who were murdered at Pilate's command while they were praying. Or the construction workers struck down by a collapsing tower. Jesus responds by challenging the assumption that God was punishing anybody. That assumption itself seemed to imply it was the questioners, not God, who were judging the victims to be guilty of something.

And so Jesus invites his hearers—that would be you and me—to examine ourselves and calls for repentance with some urgency. "Repent" does not mean "feel bad about yourself." Rather:

- Repent means return to your original created goodness.
- Repent means return to the very source of your life, to God.

- Repent means change the direction in which you are looking for happiness.
- Repent may mean letting go of something, like letting go of arrogance, of not needing God or anyone else. We don't like to admit that maybe we are not self-sufficient but in fact are totally dependent on God and on each other. Or maybe it means letting go of past hurts and misunderstandings. For some reason we like to hold on to all that even though it eats away at us inside and makes us more and more miserable. What is it about letting go that makes it so difficult? Is it that somehow we feel that as long as we can cling to our sense of being offended or wronged by someone, we feel superior to that person in some way?
- Repent perhaps means letting go of the deep-seated need to get even. We call that kind of letting go forgiveness.
- Repent maybe means letting go of the habit of putting my needs, wants, and desires ahead of anyone else's.
- Repent maybe means letting go of judgmental attitudes and prejudices.
- Repent maybe means, ironically, that we have to let go of the notion that we don't need to let go!

Repent means hope, a second chance, a fresh start. Repent means come back to the name we all received at our baptism: *Christian, Christ-like.* Of course, we can also come back to the unique names we received at baptism as well, like Peter, "Rock of faith"; or Michael, "God-like"; Raphael, "God heals"; and yes, even "gift of God."

Mother Always Loved You Best

2 Chronicles 36:14–16, 19–23; Ephesians 2:4–10; John 3:14–21

Sibling rivalry. Unless you happen to be an only child, you probably know something about sibling rivalry or the "mother always loved you best" syndrome. A friend of mine recently told me about a conversation he'd had with his sister on this subject. When they were growing up at home there had been three children: my friend, his sister (the middle child), and their little brother. Since the youngest had chronic health problems he always seemed to get all the attention, and this led to some built-up resentment, at least as far as their sister was concerned. In her adult life she finally raised the subject with her mother suggesting she had always loved one of the boys more than her. Her mother answered, "I loved you all the same. I did not love any one of you more than the others, but I tried to give each of you what you needed at the time." That expression of maternal love is the kind of love the Scriptures show God had for Israel and still has for us today.

The author writing Israel's history in the book of Chronicles does not gloss over how seriously Israel, priests and people alike, had violated their special relationship with God. They had abandoned the covenant forged in the saving events of the Exodus experience and no longer worshipped God alone. Nor did they bother to observe the Ten Commandments.

Still, God did not abandon them. Instead, God sent messengers, prophets like Jeremiah with powerful voices calling the people back. This was an act of parental love sending what was needed at the time. Unfortunately, what was needed went unheeded. When disaster struck and Jerusalem fell, the temple was destroyed and the people were led off into exile. God did not abandon them but sent messengers again, like the prophet Ezekiel, to keep hope alive. Later on, even Cyrus, the great pagan king of Persia was seen as an instrument of God's continuing fidelity to and love for his people. When Cyrus decreed Israel to be free and the people could return to their home, Israel knew it was God's hand at work.

But it is in Jesus that the depth of God's love and fidelity really shines forth. In John's gospel Jesus draws the parallel between Moses lifting up the serpent in the desert and his own crucifixion (John 3:14). We find the story Jesus refers to in the book of Numbers (21:5–9), where it recounts the incident of poisonous seraph serpents biting and killing people in the desert. The people recognize this affliction as a consequence of their straying and plead with Moses to ask God to take the serpents away. When Moses appeals to God he is directed to make a bronze serpent and mount it on a pole. Anyone who was bitten by a serpent and looked at the image Moses had "lifted up" recovered and lived.

In a similar way, John says whoever looks at Jesus crucified (i.e., "lifted up") and sees in him the incredible love God has for us will live. And not just an ordinary life but eternal life. God so loves the world that he sent his only Son because that is what we needed.

As Christians, we have a choice. We can embrace Jesus, his healing, compassion, and forgiveness and live in harmony with his own example and teaching, or we can choose not to follow. In John's terms, to follow Jesus is to live in light. To refuse to follow him is to live in darkness.

It is no accident that Nicodemus approached Jesus at night. He was a Pharisee and had a lot to lose as a disciple of Jesus. So he first appears out of the darkness. At the end of John's gospel, however, Nicodemus boldly returns in broad daylight to assist in taking Jesus down from the cross and in providing a burial for him. He has seen and is moved by the incredible love God has for him. Amazing what we are capable of doing when we are confident of being loved.

Paul says we are all "the handiwork of God" (Ephesians 2:10). Another way of putting it is that we are all "God's work of art," something in which God takes great delight and satisfaction.

When the friend I was telling you about earlier was only a year old he came down with pneumonia. It was serious. The doctor told his mother that if he made it through the night the crisis will have passed and he would recover. His mother had heard these words before—the night she lost another son to pneumonia. So she stayed by the infant's bedside every minute of the night picking him up and caring for him when he fussed or vomited and by morning the crisis had passed.

That maternal love gives flesh and blood to the love God has for each of us. God doesn't love any one of us more than another, but he remains at our side keeping vigil, constantly ready to give us whatever we need at the time … even his only Son.

Something New

Isaiah 43:16–21; Philippians 3:8–14; John 8:1–11

On March 4, 1865, President Abraham Lincoln addressed a war-weary nation that had torn itself apart for four long years in unbelievable bloodshed. As he took the oath of office for a second term, the war, though still raging, looked as though it was coming to a conclusion. In his extremely brief inaugural address Lincoln eloquently articulated the tragedy of the Civil War saying, "Both [sides] read the same Bible and pray to the same God, and each invokes his aid against the other. It may seem strange that any man should dare to ask a just God's assistance in wringing their bread from the sweat of other men's faces, but let us judge not, that we be not judged."

Then he looked into the immediate future with hope, uttering the well-known words "With malice toward none, with charity for all … let us strive to bind up the nation's wounds … to do all which may achieve and cherish a just and lasting peace" (Lincoln's Second Inaugural Address).

Toward the beginning of his speech Lincoln had alluded to all the statements and announcements necessitated by the war and said, "little that is new could be presented."

Yet the nation that was about to emerge from the Civil War was new. The Union had survived, but some said it had lost its innocence. Slavery had been banished for good and could no longer be the same bitter and divisive issue, but the wounds suffered during those years would take a long time to heal, and there is evidence even today that some scars remain. The United States that emerged from the Civil War was in many ways a new nation.

When God spoke through the prophet Isaiah, saying, "See, I am doing something new" (Isaiah 43:19), he was speaking to a people who had endured a national trauma of their own: exile in Babylon. And they were about to return to a shattered Jerusalem and start a new life. They remembered the great Exodus experience of their ancestors, who left Egypt to start a new life of freedom, yet were reminded their experience was new. This was a new Exodus.

But what does all this have to do with a gospel story linked with this reading about a group of scribes and Pharisees who drag a woman guilty of adultery before Jesus and everybody else with the intent of trapping Jesus and stoning the woman? The proverbial killing of two birds with one stone, so to speak (John 8:3–11).

It looks as though this is a trap Jesus cannot escape. If he decides the letter of the law must be followed, the woman is killed on the spot and Jesus is discredited and no longer seen as the prophet of mercy. If he argues for mercy, then he appears to place himself in direct opposition to the law of Moses and God's justice. Quite a dilemma.

How does Jesus respond? He stalls, a tactic sometimes resorted to by parents.

He doodles in the sand, which not only expresses disinterest but buys time—not to mention annoys the opposition. To their dismay, when they press the issue they find themselves caught in their own trap. Jesus responds, "Let the one among you who is without sin be the first to cast a stone at her." In essence he says, "Look at yourselves! Are you not also sinful? Do you think you do not also need God's mercy? Divine justice is one thing; human injustice is another.

In the glaring light of that stark truth the woman's accusers are forced to look inward, admit their own need for mercy, and silently slip away, humbled, if not ashamed.

Jesus had found a way to extricate the woman from a very dangerous situation, save her life, and allow her to begin over again. The stones of death and judgment had fallen harmlessly around her and she had a chance at a new life.

Great story. But maybe we ought to be a little less comfortable when we realize Jesus challenges us as well. What stones of death and judgment do we carry around ready to hurl without so much as a second thought? Are they big, damaging rocks like racism, bigotry, prejudice, or revenge? Or are they the less lethal yet hurtful stones of petty, unkind comments, gossip, and innuendo?

Maybe we need to loosen our grip on these weapons of self-righteousness, let them fall to the ground knowing we need to accept God's mercy ourselves. Might that also be the beginning of a new life?

Is Anybody Listening?

Acts 15:1–2, 22–29; Revelation 21:10–14, 22–23; John 14:23–29

A number of years ago, when I was a campus minister at a local college, one of the professors related a small incident that illustrated to him how times had changed. One day the professor spotted a student he knew walking across the campus, and in an attempt to get the student's attention, he called out and started waving his arms, to no avail. The student just kept walking along, totally oblivious to the fact someone was trying to communicate with him, all the while absorbed in the music playing through his Walkman.

Jesus promised his disciples he would send the Holy Spirit to teach them everything and to remind them of his Gospel message. Fortunately, in the first century there were no Walkmans or i-Pods or anything else to keep the disciples from listening when the Spirit did speak. To be instructed by the Spirit, one first has to be attentive to the Spirit, and that means one has to be prepared for some surprises.

As Luke tells it, it didn't take long for the surprises to show up. Almost immediately the community had to tackle an issue that never came up when Jesus was with them. The question was: Do non-Jews have to become Jews in order to be Christians? The question may sound strange to us, but it was a burning issue hotly debated in the very early church. Luke tends to write diplomatically, but even he says there "arose no little dissension and debate" (Acts 15:2) over the issue.

It must have been quite a fight, and it became such a point of contention the church held its first "council" ever, "the council of Jerusalem" (though no one called it that at the time.) And Paul, Barnabas, Peter, James, and other leaders in the community went at it, each arguing his own point of view.

What is remarkable about this is how the matter was finally resolved. Everyone came to realize that non-Jews (such as Cornelius and his whole household) were already receiving the Holy Spirit so they did not need to become Jews first. Actually, the Holy Spirit had already solved the problem and they merely recognized it, a fact illustrated in the wording of their message from Jerusalem announcing, "It is the decision of the Holy Spirit and of us not to place on you any burden beyond what is necessary" (Acts 15:28). They were attentive to what the Spirit was doing among them.

The community had weathered its first major controversy and undergone its first surprising change. It was the first of many right down to the present day. Today we too, as a church, face our own issues, challenges, and surprises and sometimes that can make one feel very uncomfortable. Yet the promise of the Spirit in the gospel and the attentive response to the Spirit by the community in Acts assure us that what matters is simply that the Spirit is still here.

We can witness that fact when members of our community are sealed with the gift of the Holy Spirit during confirmation. No one can ever judge the disposition of another person, but often those newly confirmed seem to glow with the Spirit. And then there are the youngsters who receive Jesus in the Eucharist for the first time. They may be very young, but they know something special is happening and that Jesus is there. How attentive are we to that presence ourselves?

Every sacrament is essentially a meeting between Christ and the believer. Jesus promised to be here always until the end of time. His presence is mediated through community, sacraments, Spirit, through water, bread, wine, oil and human touch.

Are we paying attention to the sacred encounter offered right here and now, or do we risk being like that student with the Walkman in his ear just going along totally oblivious to the fact that someone wants very much to reach out to us?

Remembering with Gratitude

Deuteronomy 8:2–3, 14–16; 1 Corinthians 10:16–17; John 6:51–58
Reflections on the Feast of the Body and Blood of Christ
(which in 2005 fell on the same weekend as Memorial Day)

By the end of the Civil War, six hundred thousand soldiers had died and no family, north or south, had escaped the pain of losing a loved one. The nation, so nearly shattered, was still deeply divided and severely wounded. The grief was palpable. In the area just outside Rochester, New York, the little parish of St. Ambrose lost so many of its sons in the conflict that it chose to change its name to Our Mother of Sorrows. Everyone was in mourning.

So on May 5, 1866, the townsfolk of the village of Waterloo, New York, gathered and devoted themselves to placing flowers on the graves of their war dead. In this simple gesture of honor, respect, and remembrance, the tradition began that would first be known as "Decoration Day" and later become "Memorial Day."

All during the Memorial Day weekend Taps are sounded, twenty-one-gun salutes ring out, parades are held, and speeches given all for one purpose: to remember with gratitude the sacrifices others have made for their families, for their communities, for their country, and for us. And while for many Memorial Day seems to have become little more than a day off to usher in the summer season, there is still something in this holiday that is more commemoration than celebration. There is something deeply reflective in it. All our public and private ceremonies in observance of Memorial Day serve as evidence of just how profoundly human and meaningful it is for us to remember with gratitude the sacrifice others have made that we might live.

And is that not what we do at the Eucharist? We gather into one body and remember with gratitude what God has done, and continues to do, for us that we might live. In the reading from Deuteronomy Moses urged the people to remember what God has done for them. As they stood poised to enter the land they would finally be able to call home after wandering for forty years, he told them to remember God has been with you every step of the way—through all manner of hardship and adversity, from the oppression of slavery through the

25

harsh desert with its scorpions and serpents. Remember when you thought you would die of thirst how God made water flow from rock. Remember when starvation threatened, God provided manna, a strange and mysterious food no one had ever seen before (Deuteronomy 8:2–16).

Jesus recalls that strange and mysterious food and then goes on to give it an even more profound significance: "This is the bread that came down from heaven. Unlike your ancestors who ate and still died, whoever eats this bread will live forever" (John 6:58). That mysterious bread come down from heaven is his own body. His life, his life's blood poured out for us all that we might live forever.

We remember with gratitude at every Eucharist this incredible sacrifice that has been made that we might live. When we hear at the consecration, "Do this in memory of me," we remember with gratitude. When we proclaim the mystery of faith, we remember with gratitude. When in the Eucharistic prayer we recall Jesus's passion, death, and resurrection, we remember with gratitude. When the Lamb of God is held before the community whose sins have been forgiven, we remember with gratitude. When the host is held before us at communion and proclaimed, "The Body of Christ," we see the mystery, a food that does not become part of us but rather draws us into itself and transforms us and we remember with gratitude. We are not *each* the Body of Christ, but we are *all* the Body of Christ as Paul points out (1 Corinthians 10:16–17). As we receive communion we see that human and divine life, once sacrificed for us, now placed trustingly in our own hands, and we remember with gratitude.

How profoundly meaningful it is for us to remember with gratitude the sacrifice others have made that we might live.

How profoundly human and meaningful is the Eucharist, for to celebrate the Eucharist is to remember with gratitude the sacrifice One has made that we might all share in his eternal life.

Come to Me, All You Who Are Weary

Zechariah 9:9–10; Romans 8:9, 11–13; Matthew 11:25–30
(These readings and reflections were offered on the Fourth of July weekend.)

In 1883, thirty-four-year-old poet Emma Lazarus was invited to submit a poem as part of a fund-raising effort to build the base on which the Statue of Liberty would stand. Her initial response was to decline, but then, after seeing the brutality of anti-Semitic riots occurring in Russia, she was stirred into action. The result was a fourteen-line poem titled "The New Colossus," a reference to the Colossus of Rhodes, the giant statue that stood in the harbor of ancient Rhodes and was one of the seven wonders of the ancient world. You are familiar with the last lines of her poem but here it is in its entirety:

"The New Colossus"
Not like the brazen giant of Greek fame,
With conquering limbs astride from land to land;
Here at our sea-washed, sunset gates shall stand
A mighty woman with a torch, whose flame
Is the imprisoned lightning, and her name
Mother of Exiles. From her beacon-hand
Glows world-wide welcome; her mild eyes command
The air-bridged harbor that twin cities frame,
"Keep, ancient lands, your storied pomp!" cries she
With silent lips. "Give me your tired, your poor,
Your huddled masses yearning to breathe free,
The wretched refuse of your teeming shore,
Send these, the homeless, tempest-tossed to me,
I lift my lamp beside the golden door!"

These fourteen lines have inspired Americans for more than one hundred years because they capture our character and give voice to our desires, our hopes, our dream to be a nation that is not only free but just, a nation where every person is treated with respect and dignity, a nation that values the gifts of every one of its members. Every Fourth of July we see that icon of

America—the Statue of Liberty—showered with fireworks in celebration of our nation and our life. And we are inspired once again to try to live up to all we claim to be, knowing we are not really there yet.

The words of Jesus are equally inspiring and challenging: "Come to me, all you who labor and are burdened and I will give you rest. Take my yoke upon you and learn from me. For I am meek and humble of heart and you will find rest for yourselves" (Matthew 11:28–29).

Both inspiring images call out all that is good in us and invite us to become more.

The Statue of Liberty's official title is "Liberty Enlightening the World"— hence the torch. Jesus referred to himself as "the Light of the World."

Emma Lazarus began her poem by saying how different this statue is. It is not brazen and conquering like the Colossus was. Rather, this statue is the "mother of exiles." Zechariah envisioned a king who came riding not as a conqueror but as a bringer of peace. And Jesus calls himself meek and humble of heart, not a conqueror.

The Statue of Liberty has become a national icon symbolizing ourselves and our country. She is the Republic. Jesus gathers us into his own Body and we become the Body of Christ.

In Matthew's gospel, Jesus addressed his words to oppressed people, those who struggled under heavy burdens, whatever their source. By contrast, Jesus kept it pretty simple: "Love the Lord your God with all your heart, all your strength, all your soul, all your mind, and your neighbor as yourself" (Luke 11:27).

His life served as an example of how to live out the basic commandment to love.

- It means living in an attitude of hospitality, putting aside one's own concerns to tend the needs of another. How many times in the gospels do we see Jesus doing just that, even when he is tired and in need of rest?
- It means living one's faith with courage, especially in the face of ridicule or hostility.
- It means developing an ever-deepening relationship with God. That is, after all, the sole purpose of religion in the first place. The very word religion comes from the Latin *religio,* meaning to "bind back." It means

binding us back to our original source, leading us to the One from whom we came.

At the end of the Constitutional Convention, Ben Franklin was asked by a woman he encountered on the streets of Philadelphia, "Well, Mr. Franklin, what kind of government have you given us?" He is said to have replied, "A republic, madam, if you can keep it."

We might be inclined to ask Jesus what kind of life this "yoke" of his offers us. His reply might well be, "The kingdom of heaven, if you can accept it."

Follow the Leader

Isaiah 66:10–14; Galatians 6:14–18; Luke 10:1–12, 17–20

Each year, we as a nation celebrate the signing of the Declaration of Independence on July 4, 1776, just as John Adams hoped we would, with parades, speeches, and fireworks. But the freedom formally declared that day was not automatic, nor did it come without great cost. For the next eight years the war dragged on and it might have been lost if not for the gifted leadership of George Washington, who managed to keep an army together and hope alive. But even after eight long and difficult years of fighting, Washington faced perhaps his greatest crisis of all.

A year and a half after the British army under General Cornwallis surrendered to Washington at Yorktown, peace was still not yet fully a reality and the officers in Washington's army were so frustrated they were near open revolt. They had not been paid and their pensions were in jeopardy. They had had enough and were beginning to organize, perhaps even to march on Congress.

Washington had to act. The story is told that he called his officers into a meeting on March 15, 1783, in Newburgh, New York. He faced a sullen and even hostile audience but asked for patience and promised to do everything humanly possible to resolve their complaints. He told them their patience would serve as a model for generations to come, to no avail. They remained unmoved.

Then Washington remembered a letter he had brought with him from a congressman promising a speedy resolution to the problem. He took it out but seemed bewildered at first. Then he reached into his pocket, took out a pair of eyeglasses, and apologized, saying, "I have already grown gray in the service of my country. I am now going blind." It stunned the officers. By the time he finished speaking there was not a dry eye in the room. After he left, the officers voted unanimously to follow their leader's advice.

A leader leads not only by word but by example. A leader offers a vision and extends an invitation. A leader inspires others to accept the invitation and realize the vision. That is what George Washington did.

That is what Isaiah did. And that is what Jesus did.

The newly returned exiles to whom Isaiah spoke saw only ruins, but the prophet's vision of a rebuilt Jerusalem and a flourishing people invited them to join in the process of rebuilding, knowing they already rested securely in God's lap. It was an image that inspired. That's what leaders do. They inspire.

People followed Jesus because he inspired them. When he spoke, something deep inside resonated. Something came alive. They saw him repair and even restore life. Jesus healed people physically, emotionally, and spiritually. Just being in his company gave one a sense of excitement, of vitality. Jesus breathed life into people—that's what "inspire" means. And all of this is what he called "the kingdom of God."

Maybe that phrase is too familiar to us or too "churchy" to inspire us today. The truth behind it is still the same. God is not "out there" or "up there" somewhere far away. Rather, we live in the presence of God every moment. God is in every breath, in every heartbeat. That is why Jesus told his "missionaries" to announce to those who welcomed them as well as those who did not that "the kingdom of God is at hand."

The rest of the instructions Jesus gave his missionaries boils down to advice for all of us: live with confidence in God's presence. Live a simple lifestyle. In our consumer-driven affluent society, living a simple lifestyle is not viewed as particularly attractive, but it does help us remember what matters, that we came from God and we are on our way to God. God is our source and our destiny. Come to think of it, isn't that just how Jesus lived? A true leader offers a vision, extends an invitation, and inspires by example.

It just remains for us to follow the leader.

Let Go!

The Wisdom of Solomon 9:13–18b; Philemon
9b–10, 12–17; Luke 14:25–33

For as long as I had known her, Sylvia had struggled to live the gospel message in its entirety. She often responded to the needs of others as they presented themselves: the poor, the hungry, the lonely, strangers. She and her husband had even traveled to the remote mountains of Central America to join their daughter in caring for the sick and poor. And this was when they were both in their seventies.

But one of the most difficult challenges for Sylvia was letting go of possessions. After all, she did have a fondness for shrimp and sherry! One day, Sylvia was recounting a conversation she had had with a woman who, prompted by the gospel, had decided to give away many of her possessions. She told Sylvia she had decided to begin by giving away her oriental carpet. Sylvia was shocked. At this point, I interrupted Sylvia before she could tell me what she had responded and said, "Sylvia, I hope you didn't ask for the dimensions of the carpet!" She glared at me with that bemused/annoyed expression I so enjoy and said, "No. But I did say, 'That's a pretty drastic place to begin. Why not start with something smaller … like a doily?'"

How difficult it can be sometimes to part with our treasured belongings. And that is only one part of the difficult demands Jesus makes in the gospel, demands that could be summed up as "Hate your family. Pick up your cross. And get rid of all your stuff." (What's not to love?!) If Jesus were running for president today, where do you think he would stand in the polls? Yet so many of us claim to be followers! If we were to literally follow his commands we would end up alone, suffering and naked, just the way he ended up!

So what are we to make of these harsh demands he lays before us? The key to understanding all this is found in the two mini-parables embedded in the text about the man building a tower and the king estimating his military strength against an opponent. In other words, "How much is this undertaking going to cost?" What will it cost to be a disciple?

Hate your family. Of course Jesus doesn't really mean *hate* your family.

The word translated as hate here is both a combination of Middle Eastern hyperbole and linguistic quirk that might better be understood by us today as "let go of." Let go of your family. Following Jesus meant letting go of one's family—your only safety net, the only social security at the time. That was no small demand to make! But what does "let go of your family" mean for us today? How difficult is it for parents to let go of that college student going off into the world for the first time? How difficult is it to stand at the school bus stop with your little ones on their first big day? It is not so easy to let go, is it? But we know we have to. As much as we love those in our family, we do not, we cannot possess them. Possessing grasps and holds on. Loving lets go and sets free.

Pick up your cross. The cross was not only the terrifying instrument of torture but of shame. Sometimes being a disciple of Jesus can lead to suffering and humiliation. The long history of martyrs attests to that. But what does it mean for us today? Have you ever had to stand up for what you believe? Then you know what Jesus was preparing us for. The cross can show up as a loss of popularity, a missed promotion, or even hostility.

And get rid of all your stuff. Here's where Sylvia really struggled, and honestly, don't we all? Could this command be any further from the values and messages we are immersed in every day from all sides—the Internet, TV, radio? We are constantly told, "You *need*, you *want*, you *deserve*, you *desire*, you *ought to have.*"

The message seems to be that acquiring things will bring satisfaction and happiness. That may be partially true. But will things bring fulfillment and meaning in life? Not so much.

It is discipleship that leads to fulfillment and meaning in life. But discipleship comes with a cost. Are we willing to set free those we love and not try to smother, control, or grasp? Are we ready to stand up for what we believe even if we may lose popularity? Can we refuse to allow our possessions to possess us?

Discipleship is the path to what it means to be truly, deeply, fully human and totally alive. Discipleship is the way home to ultimate happiness and fulfillment: union with divine mystery and with all those we love. Isn't that worth the cost?

Have a Large Heart

Ezekiel 33:7–9; Romans 13:8–10; Matthew 18:15–20

At the end of the last Ice Age, when I was a young student at St. Bernard's Seminary in Rochester, New York, we used to find it particularly difficult to return from Christmas vacation. Those long, dark, dreary days from January until Easter (whenever it occurred) we used to call "tunnel times." It felt like you were entering a long, dark tunnel of unbroken, monotonous routine. We rarely left the campus for more than a couple of hours each week. Radios and magazines were not permitted and nothing interrupted the unvaried daily schedule, not even blizzards and power failures. We were all there anyway, and being Catholics, we had candles and we knew how to use them.

One consequence of all this monotony and close proximity to the same people day after day was a marked increase in irritability among the student body. We soon began to get on each other's nerves. It was cabin fever squared! One year during "tunnel times," controversies really started swirling about. Practically everybody was irritated or angry over something. So a house meeting was called and all 150 or so of us assembled in the chapel. Arguments were made. Positions were defended. Grievances were aired and tempers flared. We were, in fact, generating more emotional heat than the light of wisdom we were seeking.

In the midst of all this arguing one of the students in the class ahead of me, who was unassuming, humble, and straightforward, stood up and faced the assembly. He said, "I want to ask all of you to join me in one full minute of silence. That's all. Just one full minute of silence. Can we do that?" Then he turned toward the tabernacle, bowed his head, and stood there while we were all immersed in silence for a full minute. Then he turned around, looked at everyone and said softly, "You see? At least there is one thing we can all still do together." Then he sat down.

Somehow that minute did more to defuse the tensions in the community than all the arguments, positions, and debating. Ruffled feathers were smoothed and aroused emotions calmed, at least a little bit.

Jesus knew that every community is going to have its share of conflicts, whether it is a community of two—such as a husband and wife—or a family, or a village, or a parish, or a monastery, or even a community of professed religious types who have taken a vow of silence.

Psychologist Father Ray Carey told the story of how he was once invited to a community of sisters who had taken the vow of silence to resolve conflicts there. Puzzled, he asked Mother Superior how there could be any conflicts where no one spoke. Mother Superior replied, "Father, I am now going to demonstrate to you how to tell someone to buzz off by peeling a carrot." With glaring eyes and chopping gestures she made her point.

Left unaddressed, conflicts can go on festering for a long time. They may even become grudges that die only when the person bearing them dies. Unaddressed conflicts can tear apart a community, but how to deal with them?

Jesus's solution, not surprisingly, is also a formidable challenge: talk to each other. Do not judge. Do not condemn. Do not argue. Just talk. Have a large heart and an open mind.

Easier said than done! It's much easier to complain to a third party than to actually face the one who has caused the hurt.

But here is where love, real love, the love Paul speaks about, comes in. Love is not just a warm fuzzy feeling. "Love does no evil to the neighbor, hence love is the fulfillment of the law" (Romans 13:10). Writing to the community at Corinth, another community torn apart by conflict, Paul is even more specific about love. "It is patient, kind, not all full of itself, it is not quick-tempered, and does not brood over injury" (1 Corinthians 13:4–5). In other words, love never seeks to get even, and that is the very essence of forgiveness, the basic bedrock of the Christian community.

I don't remember a single issue that seemed so very important that day back at St. Bernard's so many years ago, but I remember vividly that student bravely standing up and calling us all together in silence as he bowed his head and faced the tabernacle.

So many years later I believe that in the silence we finally heard the one voice that mattered, calling us to patience with one another and ourselves, to forgiveness and to love. It was a voice that told us that our relationship with him was reflected in how we treat each other.

The Wedding Garment

Isaiah 25:6–10; Philippians 4:12–14,19-20; Matthew 22:1–14

The only time in my entire life I have ever worn a tuxedo happened many years ago when a friend of mine from our Peace Corps days asked me to be in his wedding party. On the wedding day, as everyone was busy with last-minute preparations and the men were getting into their rented formal wear, I suddenly discovered that my tux was lacking the cummerbund. It was a little embarrassing, but what could be done? The wedding was minutes away and could not be delayed for lack of a cummerbund! So I just buttoned the jacket and made sure it stayed buttoned throughout, hoping no one would notice. And to my relief, no one did. Unlike the wedding guest in Jesus's parable who was not wearing appropriate wedding attire and was thrown out, I escaped notice and managed to stay at the party.

It is difficult to understand the motivations of a number of characters in this parable. A king throws a great feast and invites all the movers and shakers in the realm, but they inexplicably ignore the invitation. Why would they not attend *the* social event of the year, the prince's wedding? Then there were others who were invited and reacted in a still more puzzling way—they grew violent toward the king's servants. In response to such outrageous behavior their city is burned down and the king invites to his feast anybody who will come. But even then the strange behavior is not over. The king encounters a guest at the feast who insults him by not wearing the proper attire, which, like the tux, would have been provided for him.

So what are we to make of this strange story? We know right out that the kingdom of heaven is like the feast. God is the king. The servants are the prophets who are—as they always have been throughout Israel's history—either ignored or mistreated. The destruction of the city probably refers to the total destruction of Jerusalem that took place in 70 AD when the Romans burned it to the ground and completely leveled the temple.

Then the king invites another group of guests, very different from the first. These guests come from anywhere and everywhere without regard to pedigree, social status, wealth, or connections. Among them are rich and poor, Jew and Gentile. It is among these guests that the king encounters the rude person not wearing the proper attire.

What is this all about? Every parable is a challenge and this parable seems to issue not one challenge but two: if you want to participate in the kingdom of heaven you have to accept the invitation. And once you have accepted the invitation you need to act appropriately.

Initially we accepted the invitation at our baptism, and incidentally, it was at our baptism that we received our "wedding garment" in the robe given to us. At that time we were told, "You have become a new creation and have clothed yourself in Christ. See in this baptismal garment the outward sign of your Christian dignity ... bring that dignity unstained into the everlasting life of heaven." In other words, "Wear this wedding garment into the feast of the kingdom of heaven." So how do we do that?

When we come to the Eucharist, a foretaste of the banquet of heaven, we accept the invitation. When we read or listen to the Scriptures in a way that allows them to move us and even change us, we accept the invitation. When we leave church and treat others with respect, compassion, patience, and understanding, we wear the wedding garment we received at baptism. When we listen to one another without judging we wear the wedding garment given to us at baptism. When we comfort one another, encourage one another, or forgive one another we wear the wedding garment given to us at baptism.

Every day as we try to live by loving God and neighbor as we were called to do at our baptism, we accept the invitation and put on the wedding garment—and this time the cummerbund is not missing.

Whose Image Is This?

Isaiah 45:1, 4–6; 1 Thessalonians 1:1–5; Matthew 22:15–21

One day when I was quite little—I must not have been much older than six—Mom found herself just a little short in paying the paper boy, or maybe it was the milkman; I really don't remember. Anyway, she asked me if she could borrow a dime from me, careful to explain that "borrowing" meant I would get the dime back in a few days. Eager to be of help I went to my little jar of coins and found a Mercury head dime (that's how long ago it was!), which I gave her. Several days later, true to her word, Mom gave me my dime back. But there was a problem. This dime had Roosevelt's likeness on it, not Mercury. I was devastated. I complained that she didn't really give me my dime back. This was another dime! Mom tried to explain this dime was worth just as much as the other one, but I would have no part of it. This was probably my first introduction to the fascinating world of economics, a world where I still feel at a loss. Anyway, the bottom line here was that the image on the coin meant more to me than its actual value.

Jesus, on the other hand, used the image on a coin to lead people to consider a much deeper value than the mere face value of a coin. That unholy alliance of Pharisees, guardians of religious propriety, and Herodians, supporters of the Roman puppet King Herod, came to him and asked with feigned innocence, "Is it lawful to pay taxes to Caesar, or not?" The question sounds straightforward enough, but this was, as Matthew warns us, a trap set between religious conviction and political expediency. Say no and you get into trouble with the Roman authorities. Say yes and you lose all credibility with your own people. It seems like a no-win situation for Jesus—just what his enemies were looking for. Church-state matters often seem to place the two in direct opposition, or at least in an uneasy tension. We can certainly relate to that. A display of the Ten Commandments is ordered removed from a courthouse. A president recommends a Supreme Court nominee, citing the church she attends. There is heated debate over the phrase "under God" in the pledge of allegiance, and of course, the annual argument over Christmas decorations on public property—just to mention a few examples in our own time.

Sometimes it leaves one wondering if there is any solution to all the controversy, and sometimes, I must admit, I wonder if there's any such thing as "common sense" any more. Jesus does not give us a direct answer to solving the church-state debate. It doesn't appear he was interested in solving that question, but he was interested in people's hearts.

He knew the hearts of these treacherous flatterers so he decided to engage them in their own game. He simply asked them to show him the coin needed to pay the tax. Someone handed him a coin. Uneasy glances were exchanged. No one was supposed to be carrying one of these coins. No one was supposed to possess a "graven image," like a coin depicting an emperor, especially an emperor who made claims to divinity! To emphasize the point, and possibly to increase their discomfort, Jesus asked, "Whose *image* is this? And whose inscription?" "Caesar's," they admitted. So, flipping the coin back at them, he said, "Then give to Caesar what belongs to him." If it bears his image, then it must belong to him.

Then Jesus took the discussion to a whole new level when he added, "But give to God what belongs to God." There wasn't a person there who could have missed his deliberate reference to the Scriptures and their account of God's creation of human beings, "So God created humankind in his image. In the image of God he created them" (Genesis 1:27).

In his response Jesus not only destroyed their clever trap, he turned the tables on his adversaries—as he so often did and forced his questioners to ask themselves, "What belongs to God?" Still stinging from the embarrassing lesson of the coin they knew that what bears God's image belongs to God. Since the Scriptures tell us every human being bears God's image, then every human being belongs to God, even Caesar.

But where does all that leave us? Where do we discover God's image? Look at your neighbor. Look at your wife, your husband, your sons and daughters, your parents, and you will see God's image. Whether you recognize it or not is another question. I used to suggest that we all ought to write out Jesus's question, "Whose image is this?" and tape it to the bathroom mirror, but as I have aged I have come to realize that isn't necessary. As I get older, every time I look in the mirror I find myself asking, "Whose image is this?"

Can we discover God's image in ourselves? And how do we give back to God what belongs to God?

What we do at Eucharist is the first step toward the answer. We give God our lives, place them on the altar, entrust them to divine, transforming hands, and wait to receive them back as the Body of Christ. Then we go out and try to live as God's image in the world, in generosity, gratitude, compassion, and even self-sacrifice. That's how we give to God what belongs to God.

What's in a Title?

Malachi 1:14–2:2, 8–10; 1 Thessalonians 2:7–9, 13; Matthew 23:1–12

I made Bill's acquaintance many years ago in Southport, Connecticut. One day as we were strolling along the beach road in his new neighborhood, he told me about an incident that had recently happened to him in the local post office. He was having a difficult time with a less-than-congenial window clerk when someone who knew Bill came in and greeted him, saying, "Hi, doctor, how are you?" Bill was a psychiatrist. He returned the greeting, and when he turned back to the clerk at the window the clerk said, "You're a doctor? How can I help you?" The change in the clerk's attitude was dramatic. All because of a title. It really annoyed Bill. In fact, that's why he was telling me the story, just to vent a little. Why, he wondered, did it make any difference that he was a doctor? Didn't every customer deserve courtesy and service no matter who they were?

I have had similar experiences when people call me "Father." I once had a conversation with a friend whom I have known for years who insisted on calling me "Father" even though I told him it was perfectly all right to call me Ted. After all, I told him, it is what Mom and Dad call me. But he responded, "No. I'll continue to call you 'Father.' You've *earned* it." I think I understand what he meant by that—recognizing the years of seminary training, the studies, the spiritual formation, and finally ordination. And I certainly wasn't about to argue with him. I respected his point and recognized in it a deep respect for the priesthood itself. But the fact is I didn't earn the title "Father."

No one does and no one can. The practice we have in the church of using the title "Father" is really a way of recognizing the gift of a vocation that has been given—not to the individual, but to the community.

The title "father" that we use today really has no connection with the title Jesus spoke of in the gospel (Matthew 23:9). Remember, Jesus was living and speaking in a culture on the other side of the globe two thousand years ago. The title meant something quite different at that time and in that culture. The term "father" was reserved for a very few highly regarded and respected elders in the community and for those towering figures from their history such as Moses and Abraham. For example, you may remember the parable Jesus told of the rich man and Lazarus. Both of them died and Lazarus went to Abraham while the rich man found himself on the other side of the eternal abyss. When he spotted Abraham far off he called out, "*Father* Abraham!" (Luke 16:24).

But for us today, the title "father," just like any other title—professor, doctor, officer, judge, congressman, councilwoman—defines a relationship to the community. When you think about it, a title defines service more than status. In the gospel Jesus warns that it is when we lose sight of that fact that we run into trouble. When we invoke titles to gain prestige, to draw attention and admiration to ourselves, or to make ourselves seem more important than others, we actually begin to diminish ourselves spiritually. People wrapped up in themselves make very small packages.

That is precisely what Jesus warns against when he blasts certain scribes and Pharisees who do everything to draw attention to themselves. They exaggerate their prayers. They enlarge the tassels and devotional scrolls attached to their prayer shawls for show. They vie for the places of honor at public places. They play the role of spiritual leaders, but they are only *actors* (the Greek word is *hypocrites*).

So Jesus warns, do not get seduced by titles or any other form of self-centeredness. If you are looking for fulfillment, satisfaction, and happiness through self-serving titles, you will end up unfulfilled, dissatisfied, and unhappy, not to mention very lonely. All this business of honor, prestige, and titles is really just a self-destructive ego trip that leads nowhere.

True spirituality is always about connection with God, with others, with the many dimensions within ourselves and with creation. The way to honor that connection is through humility and service.

Humility is not a sense of worthlessness or a denial of our own talents. Not only is that not true, it is a lie. Humility is recognizing the truth about ourselves. Humility is the recognition of a gift *as* a gift. We do have gifts. We have talents and abilities. But they have not come from ourselves. They have been given to us for a reason—to give to others. It is all about connection.

When we are in tune with the fact that we have gifts to give as gifts we become a conduit of grace, first receiving and then giving our gifts.

Service is the active result of humility. It is the use our gifts for the benefit of others. Service actually draws us out of ourselves and any tendency to self-centeredness into the world of relationship. That's what lies behind Jesus's remark, "The greatest among you is the servant of all"(Matthew 23:11).

When we recognize our gifts in humility and put those gifts in service to others, we enter into a deeper sense of just how interconnected we all are, and that is true spirituality.

The bottom line is this: if there is any title that we have been given, a title that sums up the call of the gospel today to humility and service, a title that leads not to dissatisfaction and loneliness but to a deeper and richer experience of human life, then it is the title each of us was given at baptism, the title of "Christian."

What Do You Say When the World Has Ended?

Malachi 3:19–20a; 2 Thessalonians 3:7–12; Luke 21:5–19

A priest friend of mine once told me about a visit he had made to a woman who had recently lost a loved one. Her grief and sense of loss and loneliness had been devastating, but she confided to my friend that her pastor had come by and brought her great comfort and consolation. She went on to praise the pastor for his words of wisdom and how he seemed to know exactly what to say. She couldn't say enough about how his words comforted her. They were so wise and meaningful. Always eager to learn what anyone could say in the face of such a loss my friend just had to ask, "What did Father say?" With a tone of deep gratitude the woman replied, "He said, 'These things happen.'" It turns out it wasn't his words that were so comforting, it was his presence in her loss and grief.

When Jesus said, "These things are bound to happen" he was speaking on a much larger scale: wars, earthquakes, famine, plagues, persecutions. It's all bound to happen. And it has: Afghanistan, Syria, Iran, and Pakistan are either already plunged into war or are teetering on the brink. People are starving in sub-Saharan Africa, and poverty and hunger are still serious problems both worldwide and here in America. HIV and AIDS continue to infect thousands. And in many places in the world people are persecuted for their beliefs. The polar icecaps are melting at an alarming rate and hurricanes, tornados, and floods are becoming more powerful and more numerous.

It's all very frightening and can cause no small amount of anxiety. We might even ask ourselves, "Are we living in the 'end times'?" Maybe. Maybe not. Before we become too alarmed we need to remember something else Jesus says. "When you hear about these things, do not be terrified" … and don't listen to those who claim to know the details of God's plan. They don't.

What we do know is this: all creation rests firmly in God's hands. The act of creation is still going on. The entire universe is a dynamic place alive with change and is unfolding according to God's plan. That includes each one of us whose lives rest in divine hands, and not one of us is about to slip through God's fingers.

That is the kind of assurance in which we are to live our lives each day. In Jesus's own words, "By you perseverance you will secure your lives." Perseverance and patience are not popular virtues these days. We want everything now. Waiting makes us "antsy." We don't like to wait in lines, in traffic, for the computer to respond. Yet we are called to perseverance, a kind of steadiness, a confidence in God that no matter how scary it gets, God is still in control.

Perhaps we occupy a unique moment in history to more keenly appreciate the imagery in Luke's gospel. In the year 70 AD, after four years of war and a two-year siege of the city of Jerusalem, the Roman army broke into the city and burned it to the ground. Then, with considerable effort, they took every single stone from the temple building and tossed it over the edge of the foundation leaving absolutely nothing standing. It was the end of a world for the Jews. The temple, the focal point of their religious life, was gone forever.

On September 11, 2001, we witnessed two towers in the heart of New York City collapse into a heap of rubble in a matter of minutes, taking three thousand lives with them. It was the end of a world for us as well.

But then came the first responders, rescue workers, and volunteers combing through the wreckage looking for survivors, recovering bodies. These were living, breathing models of patience and endurance. There were no words that could express the grief. There were no words that could capture the shock. There were no words that could remove the pain so many felt. There no words that could adequately offer comfort. But their presence somehow did bring some kind of consolation and sense of care, not unlike the pastor whose presence, not his words, brought comfort to a grieving parishioner.

Where does this leave us? As Christians we look for the kingdom to eventually dawn, when suffering, pain, and grief will be wiped out. In the meantime, all we can do is try to live each day in faith, hope, and love, fully aware of the fragility of human existence and of the world around us.

Resurrection: New Life Really Is New

Easter

Many years ago, when my grandfather was still farming in the heart of the Finger Lakes region, a young, inexperienced farmer began working a nearby field. He had planted beans and they were just beginning to sprout. You've probably seen emerging seedlings like these, with the stem bent back into the soil just before the plant lifts up its head and opens, dropping the outer shell and beginning to grow. At that stage it looks like the seedling is making a U-turn into the soil. One day, my grandfather was visiting his neighbor and noticed the sprouting crop. He commented with the dry humor one often finds in the country, "Looks like you planted your beans upside down." He didn't think any more of it until soon afterward he spotted his novice neighbor plowing under his entire emerging bean crop. Evidently he just didn't know how his new bean crop should look as it came up. He didn't recognize that this new life was emerging exactly as it should.

At Easter we surround ourselves with symbols of new life bursting out all around us. The chick or duckling cracks open the shell of the egg. The tulip rockets out of the soil and bursts into colorful bloom. The butterfly struggles free of the chrysalis. And the seed breaks open its shell and sprouts from the earth.

Easter eggs, chicks, ducklings, butterflies, flowers and, yes, even jelly beans are all symbols of new life. But they are more than mere symbols. They express our hope and faith that our present life here on Earth with all its joys and exhilarations, sorrows and pains will ultimately be transformed into a new life, an expanded and far more vibrant life than the one we know now. We call it resurrection and it lies outside our experience and beyond our imagination.

That's why Mary Magdalene and her companions were at first puzzled at the empty tomb on Easter morning, and then terrified when they encountered angels announcing the incredible—that Jesus was alive. Not dead; not buried. The stone that had sealed the tomb lay as evidence that even a solid rock tomb had not been strong enough to contain the vibrant power of Jesus's risen life.

It may as well have been an eggshell. Perhaps to prepare them for this very moment Jesus had said, "Unless the grain of wheat falls to the ground and dies it remains just a grain of wheat, But if it dies it brings forth a rich harvest" (John 12:24). Jesus knew resurrection, by definition, lies beyond the scope of our limited human experience and even our considerable imaginations, so he used examples drawing from our experience.

Still, on Easter morning, the women who intended to lovingly embalm the dead body of their friend and teacher were unprepared for this development. Not to mention the apostles, who just simply thought the whole story about angels and rising from the dead was "nonsense." Even Peter, after visiting the empty tomb, went home amazed but confused.

It would take some time for this new reality to sink in. And it would take more encounters with the risen Jesus to confirm and reassure the disciples that Jesus had, in fact, been raised. But eventually they became convinced that Jesus had been raised, and that, while the news seemed improbable at best, nevertheless it was true: Jesus has passed through death to a new life. The Lord is risen.

What makes all this so exciting is that we will too! I had a brief conversation one Sunday morning before Mass with a man who was wondering out loud about resurrection. He concluded his thoughts with "Well, I guess we just don't know, do we? No one has ever come back to tell us."

To which I replied, "Well, one has."

All in the Family

Sirach 3:2–7; 1 John 3:1–2, 21–24; Luke 2:41–52

Margaret, a single mom, was not having a good day. Her three teenage daughters seemed to be taking turns having their own personal crises. With one it was relationship issues, with another it was money problems, and with the third it was all about maturity and responsibility. There seemed to be no end to the troubles that demanded attention. So when I ran into Margaret that day and asked her how she was, she just heaved a huge sigh of frustration and said, "I don't know what I'm going to do. These kids! I just get one straightened out and another one makes me crazy!"

Mary and Joseph had each other and they only had one son, but one teenager was enough to make them crazy. The only story we have of Jesus between his infancy and the beginning of his adult ministry is the story from Luke's gospel of Jesus as a child of twelve. He had been inadvertently left behind in Jerusalem by Mary and Joseph, but the story clearly shows his humanity. It is not unusual for the teenage years to be difficult for both adolescent and parents. Growing into mature adulthood presents all sorts of issues—identity, separation, rebellion, responsibility, and belonging. Sometimes they even conflict with each other. Jesus, being a normal human adolescent, was not immune to this difficult stage of growth. In fact, his actions here are quite typical: first he decides on his own to stay behind in Jerusalem without telling either parent, and then, after causing them to search for him everywhere in a state of great anxiety if not panic, he asks, What's the big deal?

On the one hand, this is a thoroughly human story and we can easily understand and even feel Mary and Joseph's growing frustration, worry, and anxiety as they search for their "lost" son. And yet we can also understand young Jesus eager to strike out on his own in the world as he grows into his own self-understanding.

On the other hand, Luke has very skillfully woven another pattern of meaning into the fabric of this most human story. The three days Jesus is "lost" in Jerusalem could very well foreshadow the three days his body is sealed in the tomb. Being "lost" in Luke's gospel often means some form of death. The prodigal son's father rejoices when his son returns saying, "For this son of mine was dead and is alive again; he was lost and is found" (Luke 15:24). Angels ask the women at the empty tomb on Easter Sunday morning, "Why do you seek the living among the dead?" (Luke 24:5) and young Jesus asks his parents, "Why were you looking for me? Did you not know that I must be in my father's house?" (Luke 2:49).

With that question Luke brings the two levels of this story together. In Jesus, whose birth we celebrate at Christmas, we have entered a new relationship with God. The One he calls Father is also our father. We are all children of the same divine Creator and so we are all members of the holy family, a fact driven home at every Eucharist as we join hands and pray the prayer Jesus himself taught us. It begins with "*Our* Father."

We may not understand one another. We may not always agree with each other. We may mystify and even irritate one another. But the fact remains that as children of the same divine Creator we are all members of the holy family. Can we reflect that reality in the way we treat each other?

Feast of All Souls

The Wisdom of Solomon 3:1–9; Romans 6:3–9; John 14:1–6
November—a Time to Remember

My good friend and pastor Father Tom Reddington used to bake bread every Tuesday morning and then give it away to the homebound of the parish as well as anyone who happened to show up at the door that day. Word soon got around that Tuesday was the best day to get a Mass card.

That was only one way Father Tom cared for and about people. He had been a military chaplain before founding Holy Name of Jesus parish in Greece, New York. When he was named pastor of this newly constituted parish, the first thing he did was throw a big party for everybody. He wanted to meet everybody and wanted people to meet each other. Tom brought people together. It was always a treat to be invited to his many dinner parties, where he took great delight in preparing and serving the meal. There was always a place at Tom's table. It was so humbling the night of my ordination when he knelt at my feet and asked for my first blessing. The next day I was deeply honored when he preached at my first Mass.

Tom was genuine, unassuming, and generous. He had a love for the liturgy and took great pride in celebrating well. In fact, celebrating, whether liturgically or more informally with friends, was life-giving to him.

Tom also had a wicked sense of humor. I remember one occasion when he stood out in the front yard of the rectory to dedicate a tree parishioners had planted in his honor. He stood there with Martin his Irish setter by his side and told everyone how honored he was and that he would remember them every time he, and Martin, visited the tree.

It was a shock and terrible sense of loss when Tom and Martin were killed in an automobile accident on Valentine's Day 1985. But his memory is still alive to me.

In the parish of St. Vincent de Paul, Churchville, New York, it has been the custom for members to bring in photos of their deceased loved ones, which are displayed throughout the church all during the month of November. Photographs are powerful. Each photo is a window into a lifetime of stories and relationships. They have a way of making a person present to us even if that person is far away or even deceased.

But there is a much more powerful link to those we love and who have loved us, a more immediate connection. And we have that connection every time we come to Mass. Every time we gather for the Eucharist, those who used to come to the table with us still meet us here at the table. We believe they are present.

It is not just their photograph. It is not just their memory. They are present. In the gospel, Jesus promised to go and prepare a place and then bring us home to it. That place is at the table of the Eucharist, and the altar I am fond of pointing out is much larger than it appears to be; it extends clear into eternity. And all our loved ones are there sharing the same meal, the same life. They are not gone or missing; they have just moved to the other end of the table.

In the second Eucharistic prayer of the Mass we hear the words "Remember also our brothers and sisters who have fallen asleep in the hope of the resurrection …" That is the time we remember our loved ones who have died, and I remember Tom, who loved baking bread and giving it away, who brought people together and celebrated life and liturgy with equal enthusiasm, and who is there at the table again with me. Who are the family and friends you remember?

Pick Me Up!

Isaiah 60:1–6; Ephesians 3:2–6; Matthew 2:1–12

It was New Year's Day and a large part of the extended family had gathered to celebrate not only the beginning of a new year but our mom's ninetieth birthday. The house was really rockin' as grandchildren ran from room to room and adults visited with each other, circulating plates of food and in general keeping the lid on the children's enthusiasm. In the midst of this benign chaos one of my niece's boys came to me, looked up, and with arms outstretched said, "Pick me up!" It was a command difficult to refuse. I picked him up and held him for a few minutes, realizing how much heavier he had become since I'd baptized him seven years before. His two brothers were soon standing there, arms outstretched and issuing the same endearing command, "Pick me up!" How could anyone say no to a child's irresistible impulse to be embraced?

Maybe that's why God chose to first come to us in just the same way, as a child, arms outstretched in a universal embrace with the same endearing, implied plea, "Pick me up!" Who could refuse? God had already tried other approaches to humanity—a burning bush, thunder and lightning, earthquakes, a fire-filled sanctuary—but they all seemed to inspire not only awe but also fear. If the Messiah, the Anointed One, the Christ was to draw people to himself, if the Christ was to attract people, lead people, and bring them together without fear, a different approach was needed.

So when Jesus was born of poor parents in another man's shelter, is it any wonder no one was expecting it? This was certainly not the kind of Messiah anyone had expected and probably not the kind of Messiah the magi had heard about. Yet the magi, foreigners, non-Jews, were the ones to recognize the Christ child when he came. The magi saw God in this child and honored him while the majority of his own people missed him altogether.

What irony. The whole story is filled with irony though we might miss it because the story is so familiar to us.

The magi had only a star to guide them. God worked through the natural world and they paid attention and responded. Herod, on the other hand had all the sacred Scriptures at his disposal, yet he refused to be moved at all.

The magi actually sought out the wisdom and guidance of the Scriptures, though not from their own tradition. Herod consulted the Scriptures only to thwart God's plan.

The foreigners would embrace Jesus. They "picked him up." The Jewish establishment, for the most part, rejected him. It is all an ominous foreshadowing of just how Jesus's life would come to an end.

What message might Matthew and the magi hold for us? One thing is clear: we are all held in a universal embrace by God, Jew and Gentile alike. God has picked us up. No one is left out. It is Matthew who tells us later, when a Roman centurion asks Jesus for help, Jesus remarks, "many will come from east and west and will eat with Abraham, Isaac, and Jacob in the kingdom of heaven" (Matthew 8:11).

So we might check our own attitudes and actions. Whom do we exclude, ignore, or overlook? Whom might we consider "outsiders" and not treat with respect, warmth, and hospitality? In other words, in whom might we miss the very manifestation of God?

That's what *epiphany* means, the manifestation of God. Where does that happen for us? This gospel story tells us God is manifest in human life in the most ordinary ways: a star in the night sky, the birth of a child.

- Whenever we are awed by the immensity of the night sky or fascinated by the delicately perfect symmetry of a snowflake, God is manifest.
- Whenever our hearts are melted by a puppy asleep in our lap or a kitten trying to untie our shoelaces, God is manifest.
- Whenever parents look in on their children peacefully sleeping in their beds, God is manifest.
- Whenever lovers look into each other's eyes and see their own love reflected back to them, God is manifest.
- Whenever a child shows up at our knees and demands in total trust and childlike enthusiasm, "Pick me up!," God is manifest.

God is manifest in many ways every day. The challenge is two-fold: Can we be sensitive enough to see it as the magi did? And can we respond as they did, opening our treasures—not gold, frankincense, and myrrh but simply our own hearts?

How Tempting

Genesis 2:7–9, 3:1–7; Romans 5:12–19; Matthew 4:1–11

I once saw a cartoon depicting two figures, male and female, standing on either side of a tree with a serpent twined in its branches. The woman was holding an apple in her hand. Slightly off in the distance stood a rocket ship with an astronaut frantically waving his arms and running toward the couple shouting, "Wait!"

Isn't that exactly the way we feel every time we hear the story of Adam and Eve's bad choice? We know how the story goes, but somehow, like watching *Romeo and Juliet*, we hope it will turn out differently this time. Of course it never does.

We think to ourselves, if only they had resisted the temptation. If only they had been satisfied with all they had. After all, they had everything they needed. They could eat the fruit of any tree in the garden, except one. They had their freedom. They had their innocence. And they had an intimate relationship with God. Wasn't that enough?

It seemed to be, at least until the serpent showed up and presented the idea that they could be more than just human. They could be like gods. And we all know how that turned out!

Throughout the centuries there have been various ways to identify or name this "original sin." Some have said it was a sin of disobedience. Others said it was a sin of pride. Whatever else it may be, it seems clear that Adam and Eve forgot the goodness of their own humanity as well as their intimate relationship with God. Maybe that is the reason we find this story so compelling.

The story of Adam and Eve is, in fact, our story. It didn't just happen long ago. It happens every day. And the garden of Eden is not a place that existed long ago and far away but lives in our own hearts. How often we forget our own goodness, that we do, in fact, reflect the very image of our Creator and that God is with us and still walks with us in the garden in the coolness of the evening (Genesis 2:8). It seems so easy to forget that being human is good and that we are already loved by God. When we forget our own goodness a deep void starts opening up inside, a hole of some kind. So we try to compensate by looking for something to fill the hole. We may try to accumulate more and more things, more wealth, more power and influence, more attention or more comforts and pleasures, as if any of these things could bring us fulfillment or make us happy. Sooner or later our eyes are opened, just as Adam and Eve's were and we realize that every one of these promises turns out to be empty, a fake, a dead end. We find ourselves disillusioned, unfulfilled, naked.

But the gospel story of Jesus facing down temptation in the wilderness would have us know the situation is far from hopeless. When Jesus was immersed in the waters of John's baptism in the Jordan River he immersed himself in our humanity. That is what we celebrate with such enthusiasm every Christmas—God becoming fully human. Now that immersion in our humanity becomes even more graphic. Jesus went down into the waters where people's sins had been ritually washed away and came up from those waters carrying our human condition—all our weaknesses, failures, limitations, even our sinfulness. It was at that point that the voice came from heaven declaring him to be the "Beloved Son," a pronouncement even Jesus probably needed to hear just then. Then the Spirit who had just descended on him like a dove led him out into the desert to be tested. Jesus went into the desert, still dripping wet from his baptism and carrying all of us with him. He would continue to carry all of us right until the end.

The desert in Scripture is a place where one meets God as well as the place of testing. In this story both happen. For forty days Jesus fasted, aware of God's loving presence in him, still hearing that proclamation of the Father's love echoing in his ears, acutely aware of God's presence in his life and aware of the goodness of his own humanity. It was that awareness that would enable him to resist stepping outside his own humanity when temptations arose.

"If you are the Son of God, command these stones to become loaves of bread." Have you ever walked through the supermarket bakery just before dinner? This is a powerful temptation rooted in our need for survival and comfort. It seems innocent enough on the surface. What harm is there in eating a little bread, especially after such a rigorous fast of forty days? But in reality this is anything but innocent. This is the temptation to step outside the very humanity Jesus has assumed, embraced and in which he has chosen to be totally immersed. This is the temptation to use power for entirely self-serving purposes and therein lies the trap. Jesus doesn't buy it.

So the Devil goes to 'Plan B': "If you are the Son of God, throw yourself down." Imagine the stir you will create when legions of angels rush to your aid and save you as you land softly on the ground. What a dazzling entrance that will be! Just think of all the attention you will get as the crowds gather around you in awe and wonder. Instant name recognition. What politician wouldn't want that? What a jump start to your ministry that would be. It is tempting to seek fame and applause. We all like to be appreciated and noticed. We do like to grab the attention from time to time and all of us want that fifteen minutes of fame Andy Warhol said we are entitled to. But at its heart it is nothing but a self-centered promise. Jesus doesn't "fall" for it.

So the Devil tries another approach. "I'll give you all the kingdoms of the world if you will worship me." That's just flat out idolatry, but let's face it, the temptation for power and control over others is really attractive, isn't it? Wouldn't we all like to have just a little more power in our lives? Wouldn't we like to have more influence and even control? I have a classmate who every now and then fantasizes what it would be like to be bishop. "If I were bishop, things would be different!" It is tempting. But Jesus sees this temptation to power as just another dead end.

Jesus didn't come to control people. He came as a servant to wash our feet and to teach us to wash one another's feet. He didn't come to get applause and to draw attention to himself for its own sake. He did come to draw us to himself so that he might offer us all to the Father. And he didn't come to turn stones into bread. He came to *become* bread for us. In short, he came to give himself to us and for us. He came to give us a share in God's life, the very thing Adam and Eve desired yet threw away. How ironic.

Jesus Himself Drew Near and Walked with Them

Acts 2:14, 22–33; 1 Peter1:17–21; Luke 24:13–35

I'd like to tell you about one of my priest heroes. I first encountered Father Bruce when I was a high school student in the minor seminary. We had each been sent out to various pastoral settings to witness priestly ministry in action. I happened to be sent to the county home and infirmary and there I met the chaplain, Father Bruce. While we were chatting and he was describing his duties as chaplain he received a call that one of the patients was dying and needed a priest. Father Bruce invited me to come along. We found the patient gasping for breath, but to this somewhat nervous young high school kid, he didn't seem to be conscious.

Father Bruce handed me the oils used for anointing and then bent over the patient, who he knew was nearly deaf. In a loud clear voice he simply said, "Bill, remember Jesus, Mary, and Joseph. Jesus, Mary, and Joseph, Bill." Then he took the oils I was holding and anointed Bill … "and Jesus himself drew near and walked with them."

Many years later, as a young priest, I found myself in an assignment filled with difficulty and adversity, none of which arose directly from ministry. Let's just say the chemistry between the residents of the rectory was far less than ideal. As luck—or more probably divine grace—would have it, that same Father Bruce used to come to help out with the Masses. So he usually stayed and joined us for dinner on Saturday evening.

One particularly tense Saturday evening during dinner a call came from one of the hospitals that a patient was dying. I jumped at the chance to go. To my surprise Father Bruce stood up and announced he was going with me. I told him that wouldn't be necessary, but he insisted. So off we went to the hospital. Not a word was spoken between us all the way there. When I parked Father Bruce said he would wait for me in the car. I told him I had no idea how long this was going to take, but he said it didn't matter, he would wait.

After finding the patient, praying, anointing, and seeing that there was nothing else I could do, I went back to the car and found Father Bruce waiting patiently. We started back to the rectory, again in silence. Then as we neared our destination he finally spoke. He turned to me and said, "Ted, I know this is a very difficult assignment, but you need to know I love you and support you." That was all he said … "and Jesus himself drew near and walked with them."

The two disciples on the road to Emmaus that first Easter Sunday afternoon were discouraged, depressed, even demoralized. Maybe that was why they couldn't recognize Jesus when he joined them and walked with them.

It should be a source of great consolation to know from Luke's story that distractions and preoccupations do not keep Jesus from drawing near and walking with us. They can, however, keep us from recognizing him, at least at the time.

Eventually the disciples did realize in whose company they had spent the entire afternoon. When Jesus took bread, blessed it, broke it, and gave it to them, they suddenly realized he had been with them all along.

The exquisite irony of this story is that the two disciples looked into each other's eyes after Jesus was no longer physically visible and found him present!

Whenever we gather around the table of the Eucharist and break bread, can we look back over the past week and find moments of unexpected grace, support, insight, or just plain resolve? Can we identify anyone who has shown understanding, lent support, offered help, or just listened with a sympathetic ear?

It is at the breaking of the bread we might suddenly come to recognize him and know that Jesus himself drew near and walked with us too.

Magic!

Micah 5:1–4a; Hebrews 10:5–10; Luke 1:39–45

One year, just before Christmas, a young father told me a story with great delight about snowmobiling with his five-year-old son a couple of nights before. They were riding along a trail when suddenly a deer ran across their path and vanished into the nearby woods. His son's eyes grew wide with wonder and when he got home he almost exploded with excitement telling his mom he had seen one of Santa's reindeer. His dad finished the tale with a twinkle in his eye as he said, "He'll believe in Santa Claus for a long time!"

Kids are full of anticipation, excitement, and joy as the final hours tick away until Christmas. And as any parent knows it's hard for them to contain their enthusiasm. They may even literally jump for joy. Christmas is just magical to them.

Mary and Elizabeth, two expectant mothers, were filled with anticipation, excitement, and joy when they greeted one another. John could not contain himself as he leapt for joy even in his mother's womb. But the joy of these two mothers-to-be is truly a mature joy, rooted in faith and other-centered, each rejoicing in how God has blessed the other. Neither Mary nor Elizabeth had much in terms of earthly possessions. They were poor. But what they did have was the only gift that counts, the gift of themselves. And they gave that gift freely to God and to each other. Mary undertook a risky trip to visit her cousin and Elizabeth addressed Mary as "the mother of my Lord," quite an honor. Each rejoiced in the other and how God had blessed them.

Like the child in us on Christmas eve, their excitement, anticipation, and joy could not be contained. They needed each other. They needed to give themselves to each other. We need each other and we need to give something of ourselves as well. Perhaps that's the "magic" of Christmas. Only we don't always call it magic. Sometimes we call it grace.

Drawn Together in Unity

Leviticus 13:1–2, 44–46; 1 Corinthians 10:31, 11:1; Mark 1:40–45

The lines have been drawn. The people in different regions hold steadfastly to their point of view. Confrontations are frequent. Culture clashes are impassioned and unrelenting. Dialogue doesn't have a chance because no one is willing to listen, to compromise, or to change in any way. No one is going to give an inch. The country is divided into "blue states" and "gray states." It is the eve of the 1860 presidential election, and the United States of America is headed for a break-up. Of the four candidates running for the office, Abraham Lincoln of Illinois emerges as the victor, winning an overwhelming majority of electoral votes even though he only receives 40 percent of the popular vote.

On December 20, 1860, a special convention is called in Charleston, South Carolina, which declares, "[The] union now subsisting between South Carolina and other states under the name of the United States of America is hereby dissolved."

What followed was this nation's bloodiest war, yet its new president, Abraham Lincoln, never wavered in his resolve to restore the Union. It wasn't easy to bring people together in that climate. He was attacked from all sides and called all sorts of ugly names, such as ape, baboon, traitor, tyrant, idiot, monster, despot, and lunatic—just to name a few.

He watched as the nation tore itself apart, but all through the dark days of the Civil War he never gave up hope that it could one day be restored to wholeness. Perhaps one reason our sixteenth president is so well remembered is that he struggled to be a unifier.

Jesus was a unifier as well and the gospel story of Jesus healing the leper is one example. The book of Leviticus spells out what happened to a person afflicted with "leprosy"—not what we know as leprosy today, but a nasty skin condition nonetheless. Such an individual not only endured the physical pain and suffering of the disease, but he or she had to endure the pain of isolation. No one could even come near. And to make matters worse, such persons had to further humiliate themselves by calling themselves "unclean." What misery that must have been.

So when Jesus encountered the leper and allowed him to approach in his desperation, healing in the form of human contact had already begun. But Jesus went much further. He actually touched this "unclean" man and restored his physical health. But more significantly, he restored this man to family and society, a fact implied by sending him to the priests. There is much more than a physical cure going on in this story. Often in the gospels we see Jesus uniting people to their community through healing, forgiveness, exorcism, and even parables.

Paul too is concerned with uniting the Corinthian community. The concern we read in the brief passage from his letter (1 Corinthians 10:31–11:1) is that members of the community respect each other and not shake the faith of the less sophisticated among them. It all had to do with food sacrificed to idols, but the basic concern is to unite the community and avoid divisions.

So what does all this have to do with us? We live in a world and a society marked by very deep and alienating divisions. Not long ago one could turn on the evening news and see the Islamic world in an uproar over insulting cartoons. In the West we may find it difficult to understand the outrage, but it is similar to the religious outrage the Jews felt when the emperor erected a statue of a Roman god in their temple. All images were strictly forbidden and an idol was especially offensive. They called it the "abomination of desolation." A cartoon depicting the prophet Mohammed has a similar impact on Muslims. Situations like that are only further exacerbated by political leaders who exploit the situation—certainly no unifiers there.

At home we recognize our own divisions by the familiar terms "culture wars," "red states," and "blue states." In our church there are similar deep divisions. What can we do?

We might start by taking our eucharistic prayer to heart when we pray that we "be brought together in unity by the Holy Spirit." When we pray we are not ordering take-out as if we expect God to just hand us anything we ask for. That attitude may come perilously close to taking the Lord's name in vain. When we pray we commit ourselves to work for what we ask for. We know we cannot do it ourselves and we ask for God's help. When we pray for unity we are not asking for God to change everybody else so they will get along with us, but we are opening ourselves to being changed. We express a willingness to treat others with respect, even in our differences—which leads to another point.

We might follow Paul's advice and respect one another in our differences. We might consider how we can strengthen each other and find common ground, which should be our common faith in Christ. We might consider the uniting value of true dialogue. To enter into dialogue is to express a willingness to change. It doesn't mean we lose our identity or our values, but it does mean we are willing to see things from another person's perspective. Dialogue is not a debate where we try to put forth our own ideas, convince the other side or score points. Dialogue involves careful listening, being present to the other person and allowing their words to touch us without preparing a response before they are finished speaking.

These are just a few suggestions that we might try to become unifiers. How important is it? Abraham Lincoln, Paul, and Jesus all gave their lives to bring people together. It's *that* important.

Just Have Faith

The Wisdom of Solomon 1:13–15, 2:23–24;
2 Corinthians 8:7, 9, 13–15; Mark 5:21–43

I have fond memories of my maternal grandmother, whose name was Lucy, but Grandpa always referred to her as "Lu." She was one of the world's worst euchre players, but she did make the greatest pies and cookies and she could make you laugh with her own unique sense of humor. But there was one side of Grandma that was insurmountable, and you never wanted to run up against it! She could throw a wet blanket on just about any dream and she could put obstacles in the way of just about any new project. And that explains why my grandfather undertook the incredible feat of building a cottage near the Thousand Islands without ever telling Grandma. She would never have allowed it. Grandpa would patiently gather building materials for weeks at the place where he worked, collecting scrap wood and metal printing plates he would later use for "siding," and then, when the time was right, he would call my dad to come with his truck. They would load up and off they would go for a weekend "hunting trip." At least that's what Grandma was led to believe. It was vital that she never find out what he was really up to, so every time Grandpa called Dad up to arrange yet another trip to the Islands, he always concluded with the caution, "Don't tell Lu!" This went on for years until the cottage was finally finished and Grandpa took Grandma up to see and enjoy it herself. It was hard even for Grandma to throw a wet blanket on a completed project.

It has become family legend how Grandpa managed to deal with Grandma's negative attitudes and wet blankets. When they celebrated their fiftieth wedding anniversary, everyone agreed their secret of success could all be attributed to three little words: "Don't tell Lu!"

In the gospel story, when we see Jairus, the worried father and synagogue official or the unnamed woman with a hemorrhage approach Jesus in their faith, we may not fully appreciate all the negative energy they had to overcome in order to trust.

Internally that negative energy may have been a gnawing anxiety that maybe Jesus could not do anything to help them. Or maybe he could but would choose not to help. The woman with the hemorrhage may well have had good reason to trust no one. After all, Mark tells us, she "had suffered greatly at the hands of many doctors and had spent all that she had" (Mark 5:26) and had not gotten any better. In fact, she got worse. Why should she trust anyone anymore? But she was desperate.

So was Jairus. Where else could he turn? And to make trust even more difficult for him, there came the devastating news: "Your daughter has died. Why trouble the master any further?" (Mark 5:35). At the house, the mourners actually ridiculed Jesus when he offered hope. In the face of it all, Jesus responds with a simple, "Do not be afraid. Just have faith." In other words, "Trust me." For the little girl and for the woman in the crowd, that trust was well placed. Both had their lives, as well as their connection to the community, restored to them.

Mark, of course, tells us this story not just because it is a great story but because it is our story as well. We too live in a world filled with internal and external negative energy. There is certainly no shortage of fear in our world, with threats of pandemic disease, nuclear war, terrorism, natural disasters, and death. There is the fear that springs from doubt about whether God is present in our lives, or cares, or even exists at all. There is the fear that maybe there is no reality beyond what we can see and measure, that maybe religion itself is nothing more than meaningless rituals.

To all these fears the Gospel responds, "Fear is useless. Just have faith." There is more to life than meets they eye, and faith is not a matter of creeds, or rules, or even beliefs. Faith is a matter of trust. Faith is a living relationship that transcends the visible world and reaches into the deepest recesses of our being where we cannot see, but what we experience there is very real. Yet, quite naturally, faith often finds expression through the very visible, tangible world of human touch. Often when that happens we call it "sacrament." The woman only wanted to touch the edge of Jesus's robe. And Jesus took the little girl by the hand. He touched her and life flowed into her again. Touch is so vitally important to us. Without nurturing, loving touch we human beings can wither and fail to thrive.

Jesus often reached out to touch people, and that same divine healing hand reaches into our lives even today. It happens at the Eucharist, and it happens in all the other sacraments as well. We are touched by God's powerful, forgiving, healing hand, and like the two women in the gospel story, we are restored to life and community. For God's hand, often felt through the medium of human touch and regularly celebrated in the sacraments, is far more powerful than all the doubts, fears, anxiety, and cynicism that poison our world. We only need to trust.

Grandpa was able to get around Grandma's negative impulses with just three little words: "Don't tell Lu." Jesus tells us we can get around much greater negative energy in our world also with three little words: "Just have faith."

Invite the Poor

Sirach 3:17–18, 20, 28–29; Hebrews 12:18–19, 22–24a; Luke 14:1, 7–14

Many years ago, when I was a student at the University of Louvain, Belgium, it was customary for us students at the American College to disperse all over Europe for summer vacation. It was always entertaining when we returned in the fall to swap adventures from those summer days. One year, two men came back with the tale of how they had been "arrested" in southern France for stealing corn. It seems these two were riding their motorcycles by a vast cornfield when they thought it might be nice to have a little corn for dinner. The farmer would surely never miss a couple of ears. Yes, even seminarians can fall prey to temptation. So they stopped and helped themselves to a few ears. But as luck would have it, just as they were returning to their bikes a police car came by. The officer stopped, looked at them holding the evidence, and asked for an explanation. When they explained they were hungry and intended to eat the corn, the officer told them to come with him. The two thought they were in serious trouble. But to their surprise, instead of going to the police station the officer took them to his home and there, in a comfortable house looking out over a beautiful valley in the Pyrenees Mountains, he treated them to a proper French dinner.

It turned out the officer couldn't believe anyone would be so desperate as to eat corn. Corn was for pigs and cows. These two young Americans must have seemed to him like the prodigal son longing to eat the pods thrown to the pigs. So he took pity on them, took them home, and seated them at his own table where he provided a meal he knew they could never repay.

He probably never gave it a thought that his actions modeled the advice Jesus once gave his host as he reclined at table with him: "When you hold a lunch or dinner, do not invite your friends or your brothers or your relatives or your wealthy neighbors in case they may invite you back and you have repayment. Rather, when you hold a banquet, invite the poor, the crippled, the lame, the blind; blessed indeed will you be because of their inability to repay you" (Luke 14:12–14). And, quite frankly, what Jesus said was not only shocking, it was downright rude. Jesus was a guest telling his host how to be a host, and his advice amounted to committing social suicide. In that culture, once you associated with those beneath your social standing no one would ever accept an invitation from you again. You would be socially ruined.

Only at the resurrection could one hope for any kind of reward. It is no accident that Luke links the advice about dinner party guests and resurrection *at* a dinner party. In Luke's gospel banquets frequently imply the kingdom. Here, Jesus clearly includes everyone in the kingdom, especially those who are weak, infirm or disabled in any way. In fact that is the very sign of the kingdom.

When John the Baptist, who was in prison, sent disciples to Jesus to ask, "Are you the one who is to come or are we to wait for another?" Luke says, "Jesus had just then cured many people of diseases, plagues, evil spirits and given sight to many who were blind and he answered them, 'Go tell John what you have seen and heard: the blind receive their sight, the lame walk, the lepers are cleansed, the deaf hear, the dead are raised and the poor have the good news brought to them'" (Luke 7:20–22).

The kingdom is a banquet where even those of most humble means are not only welcome but cared for and cared about. Whenever we find ourselves at the banquet of the Eucharist, we would do well to recognize ourselves as the poor and the weak. None of us can ever repay the gift given to us, but that is as it should be. What we are instructed by Jesus to do is to care for one another, especially those among us who are weak, suffering or struggling, physically, emotionally or spiritually. In extending our hearts and hands in welcome, inclusion and prayer we, who have known our own suffering, weakness and struggle, offer the healing presence of Christ in the community. That is a gift no one can ever repay. All we can do is respond with gratitude.

The Invisible Man

Amos 6:1a, 4–7; 1 Timothy 6:11–16; Luke 16:19–31

As a Peace Corps volunteer teaching English as a second language in South Korea, we were all given Korean names to fit into the culture a little more easily. I was so proud to be able to speak Korean, even though it was on the most basic level, to live independently and to be able to take care of simple day-to-day needs such as mailing letters, talking to the neighbors, and bargaining at the market. You simply did not buy anything at the market without bargaining first.

So when I entered the local tailor's shop to order a pair of pants, I was confident my Korean was adequate. The tailor politely listened as I told him my name and what I wanted. Then he took measurements, showed me the choices in material, and said the pants would be ready in a week.

When I returned, the pants were neatly packaged and ready to go. I paid the man, took my parcel home, and immediately tried on my new pants. They were perfect. Then I noticed some writing on the lining of one of the pockets. It said, "Mi gook" (American). That discovery left me feeling a little amused and slightly deflated at the same time. Here I had tried so hard to speak this man's language, made every effort to fit into his cultural world, and even use a name he could relate to, but he ignored it all preferring to just label me as that American, a foreigner.

But then I realized it was just easier for him to see me that way. It may have been easier, "more practical," even, but on the other hand it still felt depersonalizing. He really hadn't seen me at all. In spite of my best efforts I was not really part of his world.

Like many life experiences this was a lesson I had not anticipated. How alienating, how depersonalizing, and how lonely it can feel when, like the rich man ignoring Lazarus, no one knows your name, when no one even sees you as a person.

Marry Me—By the End of May!

Isaiah 62:1–5; 1 Corinthians 12:4–11; John 2:1–11

Pete and Peg had been dating for quite a while and were planning on getting married, but every time the subject of setting a date for their wedding arose, Pete would object that it just wasn't time yet. It's not that he had any reservations about the commitment to marriage, the problem was he wanted to be sure that everything was in order. Among other things that meant there would be enough money put aside for a substantial down payment on a house for the two of them.

Peg, on the other hand, was growing tired of what she perceived as procrastination and so she finally announced to Pete, "Either we are going to be married next May or we are not going to be married at all."

And so the happy couple was wed the following May—on the thirty-first. I am not sure if that last day of the month was a concession to Pete's need for preparation or not, but it was the beginning of a fifty-nine-year loving marriage. It might never have happened if Peg had not recognized the time was right and provided the necessary push.

At a wedding in Cana Jesus wasn't sure he was ready either. As far as he was concerned he was just another guest enjoying the celebration. When his mother informed him there was an embarrassing shortage of wine he didn't want to hear it. "So what do you want me to do? I'm not ready." But, like Peg, Mary was not about to accept this foot dragging. Somehow she knew his hour *had* come. And, also like Peg, she issued an ultimatum—not directly to Jesus but to the servants. "Do whatever he tells you." Then she simply walked away, leaving everything in his hands. What a way to be put on the spot—left standing there with all the servants staring expectantly, waiting for directions.

Maybe it's because this story is so familiar to us and we know what happens next, with the water becoming wine and all, that we do not recognize that Mary's indirect ultimatum is, in fact, a profound act of faith.

Without that act of faith, the miracle, "this first sign" as John puts it, may never have happened. It was an act of faith that pushed Jesus into action and produced an abundance of the best wine ever. For John this miracle became a "sign" of the heavenly banquet, a sign of divinity married to humanity. We recall this union at every Eucharist as the gifts are prepared at the altar and water is added to the wine and this prayer is prayed: "By the mystery of this water and wine may we come to share in the divinity of Christ who humbled himself to share in our humanity."

It was Mary's act of faith in her son that unlocked this treasure and revealed to Jesus's disciples who Jesus was. But what is interesting to note here is just how that act of faith is expressed, not directly to Jesus, but indirectly to the servants. As Mary walks away, the implication is: it is all in his hands now. Just follow directions and he'll do the rest.

We often receive Jesus's words in the gospel as being addressed to us directly, but here it is Mary's directions to the servants that are addressed to us as well. "Do whatever he tells you." But how do we follow those directions? Jesus is not standing there to tell us to fill the water jars with water and so forth. On the other hand, he has told us what to do:

- "Do not judge that you may not be judged" (Matthew 7:1).
- "Love one another as I have loved you" (John 13:34). In other words, give yourselves to each other every day—feeding, listening, accepting, forgiving, healing. Wash each other's feet if you have to.

Care for the hungry, thirsty, lonely, naked, sick, and imprisoned (Matthew 25:31–46). Remembering that whatever you do to any of them you do to the Lord.

If we do whatever he tells us we may be surprised to find the water of our everyday human activity has become the wine of divine life and presence. It is the kind of experience that transforms an ultimatum like Peg's "Marry me by the end of May or we won't get married" into an act of faith in each other and in Christ present.

Doubting Thomas—Model of Faith

Acts 5:12–16; Revelation 1:9–11a, 12–13, 17–19; John 20:19–31

Anglican Bishop John A. T. Robinson wrote a book many years ago titled *But That I Can't Believe*. While I cannot quote exactly from his book, I do remember the way he introduced his thoughts. He wrote that when someone told him they did not believe in God anymore he would ask them to describe the God they did not believe in. Often the description would go something like this: I don't believe in a God sitting on the clouds with a long white beard who keeps an account book of everyone's good and bad deeds. I don't believe in a God who would delight in or even demand the suffering and death of his only Son. I don't believe in a God who sends suffering into human lives as punishment.

The list might vary somewhat but usually when the description was complete, Bishop Robinson would reply, "I don't believe in that God either."

That might lead to a further conversation about what faith is all about, and the observation that faith is not, nor can it ever be, an insult to our intelligence.

Faith is at the core of the gospel as John tells us in his closing words, he wrote the whole gospel "that you may come to believe that Jesus is the Messiah the Son of God and that through this belief you may have life in his name" (John 20:31).

It's Easter Sunday afternoon. The disciples are locked away in fear. Then the unimaginable happens: "Jesus came and stood in their midst." He greets them, shows them the wounds of his passion to prove it is really him, and then moves on to the important matter of mission, the mission of forgiveness in the world.

But it is Thomas who plays the role of defining faith. "Doubting Thomas" reveals faith. He cannot imagine the resurrection is real and that Jesus is alive even though the others insist they have experienced the Risen Lord. Thomas wants to see and to touch. He needs to experience the Risen Jesus himself.

And when he is surprised by just that experience Thomas backs off his demand and can only utter a profound act of faith, "My Lord and my God!"

Jesus responds by looking beyond Thomas and addressing us so many generations later saying, "Blessed are those who have not seen yet believe." In a way not often found in the gospels this story speaks directly to us and offers some insights about faith we may overlook because the story is so familiar.

- Does it mean our faith is weak if at times we are fearful? Apparently not. The disciples were afraid and locked themselves securely away even after Jesus appeared to them the first time. Later, that fear would be overcome by courage in proclaiming the risen Lord. But not just yet.
- Does it mean Jesus is absent just because we do not see him? Apparently not. John says, "Jesus came and stood in their midst" despite locked doors, but Jesus may very well have been there all along, and heard Thomas's doubts and demands.
- Is our faith weak if we cannot imagine the resurrection? Definitely not. How can we be expected to imagine something that lies so far outside ordinary human experience?
- Since we live so long after these events does it mean we cannot hope to see and be touched by the Risen Lord? While we could never experience the Risen Jesus as the disciples did on that first Easter, it does not mean we cannot see and be touched by him. When we celebrate the sacraments we encounter the Risen Lord mediated through human touch. Laying on of hands, pouring water, bread and wine, anointing with oil, and human embrace all mediate the Lord's presence.
- Does it mean our faith is weak if we doubt? Here is where Thomas really shines. Certainly not! *Doubt is part of faith.*

It was Thomas, our doubting double, who later traveled on to the east preaching the gospel. Today, Christian communities from Iraq to India trace their roots proudly to the apostle Thomas, who brought them the gift of faith. So Thomas, in all his humanity, not only teaches us about faith, he offers us hope.

A Caravan of Grace

Genesis 15:5–12, 17–18; Philippians 3:17–4:1; Luke 9:28–36

Many centuries ago the great Chinese empire, ruled by a mighty emperor, had a tiny neighbor that had managed to remain free and independent of its colossal neighbor. This small peninsula, isolated from the mainland by a mountain range, similar to the way the Alps isolate the Italian peninsula, was known as "the hermit kingdom." Today we know it as Korea. The mountains across its northern boundary probably made it too much of a bother for the emperor to invade and claim it as his domain, so the Korean king became known as the "emperor's little brother" (actually a euphemism for client state.) Every so often the king would gather up the best his land had to offer—textiles, minerals, art, produce, etc.—and send it off in a large caravan as tribute to the emperor who in return sent back a caravan ten times larger with ten times the riches. The message was two-fold: the empire is great and you need to remember your place.

In biblical terms this relationship might have been considered a covenant: a formal understanding between two parties clarifying their place and role in the relationship. The key word here is "relationship."

In our times the account of God entering into a covenant relationship with Abram may seem very strange if not just plain bizarre: animals split in two, Abram in a trance, a smoking firepot and flaming torch passing between the severed animals. What is going on here?

Four thousand years ago in the Middle East it was not uncommon for parties to seal a covenant by passing between the severed bodies of animals. It was a graphic reminder of the consequences of violating the sacred terms of the covenant. Abram fell into a *trance,* just as Adam fell into a deep sleep when God created Eve. It signifies that something deeply sacred and mysterious is about to take place.

The smoking firepot and flaming torch are the visible manifestations of God's presence. In this account only God passed between the severed animals. It is God who has taken the initiative here in entering into this covenant, and

God alone has taken the responsibility for it. God is willing to die for it. But then, one could ask, what does God have to lose? How can God die?

The answer comes in the gospel as Jesus talks with Moses and Elijah about "his exodus, which he is about to accomplish in Jerusalem." What does God have to lose? His Son. Jesus will die in Jerusalem. God again takes the initiative in reaching out to humanity, and God will stop at nothing to draw us human beings into a closer relationship.

Relationship—that is what covenants are all about. There are two covenants honored in the brilliant light of the transfiguration. Moses represents the covenant at Sinai, the giving of the law, the Torah, which is not so much a list of rules never to be broken, as a revelation to humanity of how we are made. The Ten Commandments represent the owner's manual. Our problem is often: who reads the owner's manual? Enter Elijah representing all the prophets whose role it was to call people back to the covenant, back into relationship with a loving and faithful God.

The second covenant is the "exodus" Jesus is about to undergo: his own passion, death, and resurrection. We call it the paschal mystery. The night before he died he sealed this new covenant at table with his friends. "Take this, all of you, and drink from it. This is the cup of my blood, the blood of the new and everlasting covenant. It will be shed for you and for all so that sins may be forgiven." Do this so you may be united with me forever with a joy beyond your wildest imagination. Again God has taken the initiative in reaching out to us to bring us closer into a loving relationship not only with God but with each other.

The transfiguration reminds us that grace is God's initiative. Before we get too impressed with our own accomplishments or too discouraged with our faults, we need to remember that whatever caravans of prayers, sacrifices, and good works we send to heaven, they will all be returned to us more than tenfold.

Awesome!

Isaiah 6:1–2a, 3–8; 1 Corinthians 15:1–11; Luke 5:1–11

I returned home from my theology studies in Europe on a ship that sailed from Rotterdam to Montreal. Very early in the morning on one of the last days of our voyage a fellow passenger called me up to the deck, saying, "You have to come and see this!" When I arrived on deck I found everyone gazing out over a very calm sea, attention riveted on huge mountains of ice floating majestically and silently in the gray and pink light of dawn. Someone muttered a few nervous Titanic references, but then all were silent while we watched these enormous icebergs as we passed by. The stillness of that dawn and the immensity of the sky, sea, and ice all combined to make one feel really, really small. The only word to describe that feeling is "awesome."

Both Isaiah and Peter had awesome experiences in their own times.

Isaiah had the awesome experience of a vision of heaven itself, complete with the Lord seated on his throne and fiery beings called seraphim calling out to one another, "Holy, holy, holy is the Lord of hosts!" The earth trembled, and the house filled with smoke. Certainly this was an awesome experience and Isaiah felt really, really small: "Woe is me! I am doomed. For I am a man of unclean lips living among a people of unclean lips" (Isaiah 6:5).

Peter's awesome experience began in the most unremarkable way. He went fishing—again. Even though he was the professional, and even though he had worked at his trade all night long without anything to show for it, still he was willing to give it one more try by listening to a carpenter's son, of all things! What would a carpenter know about fishing? Still, he had been sitting there listening as Jesus spoke, and there was something about him that made Peter give Jesus the benefit of a doubt. He tried once more in deep water. The result was a record catch of fish, clearly miraculous. It made Peter feel really, really small: "Depart from me, Lord, for I am a sinful man" (Luke 5:8).

But apparently feeling really, really small is not the primary purpose of these awesome encounters. That feeling just sets the stage for what happens next. With his lips purified by a burning coal, Isaiah is called to take a new direction in life as the bearer of God's word, a prophet. As for Peter, Jesus simply tells him, "Do not be afraid," and then calls him to be a disciple, leaving behind the security of his family, business, and neighbors from the village. Jesus invites Peter, the fisherman, to take a great risk and perform without a net. But before we get too smug smiling at the challenge handed to Peter, we need to recognize that the same call, that same challenge is also issued to us in the gospel.

How do we answer that call? How did Peter respond? He had just witnessed something awesome in that record catch of fish, but it meant much more than just a handsome profit in the Capernaum fish market. What Peter realized was that he was in the presence of someone who could provide him with much more than a decent living. Jesus could provide him with living itself. A good catch of fish could satisfy physical hunger for a few days, but Jesus could satisfy the hunger of the human heart forever.

It leads to the question: What is a good "catch of fish" today? Maybe it could translate into the security represented by a position of power and influence, or maybe accumulated wealth, or even the enjoyment of the latest thrills, fun, and excitement. None of these things is bad any more than Peter's security of business, family, and village was. But power, wealth, and excitement can only feed us a short while before we grow hungry and dissatisfied again.

Jesus offers life itself at every Eucharist. Just as we enter into that awesome experience of divine life taking on flesh and transforming our human lives, we recall Isaiah's awesome experience. "Holy, holy, holy is the Lord of hosts." Here is our source of life. If we are really paying attention it ought to make us feel really, really small but not afraid. Not afraid to embrace interior transformation—we call that conversion.

Not afraid to accept the divine life offered us—we call that grace. Not afraid to live the gospel values of humility, service, generosity, and love, made possible through conversion and grace. That would be truly "awesome."

Poor and Happy?

Jeremiah 17:5–8; 1 Corinthians 15:12, 16–20; Luke 6:17, 20–26

"I've been poor, and I've been rich. Believe me, rich is better." With these words, Mae West captured what our culture seems to regard as the key to happiness. So much around us in commercial advertising, in TV programs, in movies, and online seems to send the message that wealth can provide for all our material needs and desires. It can keep us entertained and maybe even make us famous. The message is that money can buy happiness, even though deep down we know it isn't true. As one anonymous wit put it: "Maybe money can't buy happiness, but it can buy so many other things that we can forget about happiness."

Jesus would not have us forget about happiness, nor does he suggest we look for it in the wrong places. Turning so many of our cultural assumptions upside down, he says it is possible to find true happiness if we are poor, hungry, even mourning or suffering. But how can that be? How can the poor be happy? How can the hungry be happy? How can those in mourning be happy? Aren't these contradictory and mutually exclusive states of being?

On the surface it would appear so, but perhaps happiness is to be found in meaning and meaning can be found in being poor or hungry or in mourning, for these experiences have the capacity to open the human heart to compassion.

Richard Katz, a clinical psychologist who has studied how healers work among indigenous people says that every healer must in some way have suffered. And sometimes suffering is what leads healers to their calling (Richard Katz, *Sacred Stories*, 256).

In her work with cancer patients, Dr. Rachel Naomi Remen leads groups of patients through an exercise where they actually touch one another in a safe, appropriate hands-on healing session. Often patients experience a sense of reverence for the life of the person with whom they happen to be partnered. Those who are usually on the receiving end of healing care have the opportunity to give a form of healing care.

Dr. Remen took this exercise to a group of doctors and she tells of one occasion when one participant whom she describes as a very handsome and intimidating successful woman surgeon in her early thirties was partnered with a male oncologist. At the close of the exercise the oncologist said at first he wasn't inclined to say much but then decided to tell his partner about his divorce and the pain he felt. She asked him where he felt the pain and he could only touch his heart. Then he lay down on the rug and closed his eyes. His partner sat beside him for a very long time without any contact between them. Finally, she placed her hand on his chest gently yet firmly. He said after a while it felt as if she were holding his heart in her hand, that she actually felt his pain and that he was not alone. He felt safe enough to let the tears flow. When he finished recounting his experience he turned to the woman surgeon and told her, "I had no idea who you were. Your patients are lucky!"

The woman doctor had tears in her eyes as she talked about those things she felt she had lost through her medical training—her gentleness and warmth. She thought that part of her had been lost (Rachel Naomi Remen, *Kitchen Table Wisdom*, 237–41).

So what does this have to do with Jesus's beatitudes? These two doctors seem to have experienced the kind of happiness Jesus is talking about. Couldn't even highly skilled professionals like these two doctors be considered among the poor, the mourning, and the suffering? And couldn't one say they were truly blessed because of the compassion they were not only able to give but to receive?

The happiness born of compassion is not the glitzy happiness of our culture, but it is more lasting, more satisfying, and more real. And maybe one *can* be poor or hungry or even in mourning and still be happy at the same time.

That They May Be One

Acts 7:55–60; Revelation 22:12–14, 16–17, 20; John 17:20–26

In an episode from the old TV series *Dr. Quinn, Medicine Woman,* an orphan train pulls into the Colorado town carrying orphaned children from the east coast. Trains like these used to cross the country making stops along the way in the hopes of finding families willing to adopt some of the children. In this particular episode a young boy on crutches and missing a leg literally gets pushed aside as the townspeople look for other more able bodied children who might be useful on the farms or in the shops. It so happened that the local blacksmith, a black man, saw the scene and a few days later he presented the boy with an artificial leg he had made just for him. As he gave it to the boy his words reflected his own personal experience of human nature. He said, "All they see is what makes you different." The blacksmith saw not what made them different but what they had in common.

It is when we are able to look beyond what makes us different and discover what we have in common that we discover our common humanity and our fundamental unity. This was the unity Jesus prayed we would have the night before he died when he said, "so that they may all be one as you, Father, are in me and I in you, that they also may be in us" (John 17:21).

We all come from the same divine source, every single one of us. We all share the same humanity. In a very real sense we share the same life and breath, so we are already one. So why would Jesus pray that we might be one? Was he praying for something different and new to happen? Or was he praying that we might begin to see one another in a new way, to recognize our common humanity, to recognize our unity, or at least start trying to live in unity?

That's easier said than done and Jesus knew it. The same night he prayed for our unity he gave us the means to achieve it in the Eucharist. In the Eucharist we are brought closer together, both to each other and to God. But that doesn't mean it is easy. We human beings like to assert our individuality, and we sometimes disagree and find it easy, almost effortless, to irritate one another. All that can create friction, which can generate no small amount of

79

heat, and that heat can lead to division, alienation, and even hostility. Who hasn't lived through that experience?

But the bread of the Eucharist still holds us together. There is an ancient document almost as old as some of the books of the New Testament books called the *Didache,* or the teaching of the twelve apostles. It describes how appropriate it was for Jesus to choose bread for the Eucharist because making bread reflects the life of the community. Many individual grains of wheat are needed to make flour and that process involves the friction of first removing the husks, then pounding the grains into fine powdery flour. Then it is mixed with leaven, kneaded, and baked in an oven. Don't we feel like we have been through something similar in some of our relationships from time to time? But the result is one loaf. This eucharistic bread is then broken up and shared by us all. Because this one loaf now holds one life we become one as we receive the Eucharist. So Jesus's prayer is realized right there at the table. That is both the consolation and the challenge of the gospel. We are already one. The Eucharist has made it so. Now all we have to do is *act* that way.

Come As You Are

Sirach 35:12–14, 16–18; 2 Timothy 4:6–8, 16–18; Luke 18:9–14

During the 2008 presidential campaign, comedian and political satirist Steven Colbert announced he was running for president, an attempt, perhaps, to use humor to poke fun at the political process already well under way. He was not the first comedian to make this move. Decades ago comedian Pat Paulsen actually attempted to mount a serious campaign for the presidency in an effort to raise issues important to him. But he was not the first either. Way back in the 1940s comedian Gracie Allen literally threw her hat into a ring to kick off her tongue-in-cheek campaign for president as the official nominee of the "Come As You Are Party."

When Jesus addressed his parable of the Pharisee and the tax collector "to those who were convinced of their own righteousness and despised everyone else," he made it clear that authentic prayer is, in fact, a come-as-you-are party.

To Jesus's original audience, long before Luke put it in writing, the Pharisee in the parable would have represented not the "bad guy" but the very model of piety and virtue. He would have been seen as someone to emulate. He began his prayer thanking God in good Jewish tradition and then went on to enumerate all his virtues and pious practices, which went way beyond what was expected of the average person by fasting *twice* a week and paying tithes above the norm.

On the other hand, the tax collector would have been despised by Jesus's audience. Tax collectors, after all, didn't just collect taxes. They bought their position from the government, charged whatever they could get away with, and kept whatever was above the sum they paid the government. Tax collectors were known for dishonesty, greed, and collaboration with hated Roman oppression. So to Jesus's listeners it was only right that this "lowlife" tax collector should stay far back, eyes downcast, beat his breast, acknowledge his sinfulness, and pray for mercy.

Then the trap in the parable is sprung! "I tell you, the latter went home justified, not the former" (Luke 18:14).

New Testament scholar and professor Amy-Jill Levine points out that the Greek text here might just as well be translated "the latter went home *more justified than* the other" (Amy-Jill Levine. *The Misunderstood Jew: The Church and the Scandal of the Jewish Jesus*, 41). That conclusion must have come as a shock. How could this be? The key can be found in one word: "justified"—a nice churchy word we hardly ever use outside in everyday life. What does it really mean? We can get a clue from how printers use the term. For example, when lines of type are all aligned against the left margin of a page the text is called left justified. In other words, every line is in the proper relationship with all the other lines on the page.

When the tax collector went home "more justified than the Pharisee," Jesus shocked everyone by asserting he was in a better relationship with God than the Pharisee. Why? Because he came as he was, no excuses, no varnish, no comparisons to anyone else. While everything the Pharisee said may have been true, and while he began his prayer by thanking God, he just did not seem to realize that everything he was and everything he had was a gift. He began by taking up his position in the temple and then "spoke this prayer to himself." His words are more self-congratulatory than thanksgiving. Besides that, he compares himself to another, rendering judgment on someone else, an activity best left to God.

Prayer is a come-as-you-are party. We need to approach God in true humility, which is nothing more or less than recognizing that everything we have and everything we are is a gift. Gratitude, not judgment, is the appropriate response to that realization. Eucharist (the Greek word for giving thanks) is a come-as-you-are party. We do not need to dress up or cover up our faults. We do not need to deny we sometimes fail to measure up to our own standards. We do not need to come to God with our hands full of our accomplishments. How can there be any room for God to fill us if we are full of ourselves?

All God wants are open hearts and empty hands. If we come to receive the host at communion in our open empty hands with that disposition of heart, our divine Host will enter and fill us. And we will go home justified, in right relationship with God and each other.

Pentecost

In recent years astronomers and astrophysicists have made a startling discovery concerning black holes, those massive, dense concentrations of matter that have such a strong gravitational pull that everything in their vicinity is swallowed up. Not even light can escape their grasp.

Up until now black holes appeared to be predators roaming the universe. All that changed when astronomers discovered that there is evidence of a black hole in the center of every galaxy. While some are actively swallowing up everything around them, others, like the one at the center of our own Milky Way, seem to have gone quiet.

But the fact that every galaxy has a black hole seems to indicate black holes play a role in creating galaxies. It appears that as these black holes absorb matter, intense energy is released. The result is an explosion of new stars swirling around the center forming a galaxy. So black holes can be viewed as an intense creative force in the universe, a force we cannot see. How could we if not even light can escape?

One scientist remarked that while no one could ever see a black hole, someday, perhaps in the near future, someone will be able to see the intense bright light that surrounds a black hole as matter spirals at incredible speed into it.

Incredible power, creative, dynamic energy, intense luminosity, yet invisible to the human eye—couldn't these words also describe the Holy Spirit, whose gift and presence we celebrate at Pentecost?

The revelation of divine presence, sometimes called a *theophany* in Scripture is often described in similar terms: thunder, lightning, roaring wind, smoke, fire—all are visible or audible signs of an invisible presence of the divine. It is a presence that is at one and the same time awesome and powerful, yet also intimate, as close as our next breath. And Jesus breathed on them his own breath and said, "Receive the Holy Spirit," the Lord, the giver of life.

Awesome. But where is the roaring wind today? What happened to the tongues of fire? Where are those newborn stars shooting out into space creating a new world, a new galaxy?

Maybe right in front of us. Paul suggests we might consider the gifts each one of us has been given (1 Corinthians 12:3–7). Your gifts may seem ordinary, but too ordinary to be a star? Look again.

One Sunday, one of the newly confirmed members of our parish was ushering for the very first time. When I remarked about it she answered with a real sense of responsibility and belonging in the community, "I have done all the ministries now, except being a cantor." A short time later she was leading the community as a cantor as well. She was indeed one of our young stars, a tongue of fire in our community.

Like the black hole at the center of a galaxy we cannot see the Spirit, but we know the Spirit is here, breathing life into us and making us stars.

Learning to See

Isaiah 49:3,5–6; 1 Corinthians 1:1–3; John 1:29–34

Learning how to draw is largely a matter of learning how to see. One exercise artists sometimes use to sharpen their ability to see differently is known as "air drawing," or drawing negative space. For example, instead of drawing a ladder-back chair, you draw the air around it, including all the spaces between the legs, supports, the slats in the back, and the surrounding space. The end result is a fairly accurate silhouette of the chair itself.

Well, one art student just was not getting the idea at all. So the teacher took a ladder-back chair and placed a very large sheet of paper behind it. Then he fastened a marker to the end of a yardstick and directed the student to stick the marker through the chair and draw the spaces on the paper. Suddenly the student got the idea and "saw" the chair in a new way.

We all have experiences like that at one point or another when we see something in an entirely different way. When John the Baptist pointed out Jesus as the "Lamb of God," he deliberately changed the way people saw Jesus.

We are so used to that title, "Lamb of God," that I wonder if we ever stop to consider what it might have meant to John's listeners when they first heard it. People brought lambs to be sacrificed in the temple on various occasions but especially on the evening before the celebration of Passover. On that night they would then go out into the courtyards of the city to roast the lamb over an open fire, eat it, and retell the story of the Exodus from Egypt.

In that story, lambs were slaughtered by Hebrew slaves in Egypt and the blood of the lambs was smeared on their doorways. As the Egyptians were suffering the death of all their firstborn, the Hebrews huddled safe behind the protection of the blood of the lamb as they ate its roasted flesh to gather strength for their long journey to safety and freedom.

This is a story of deliverance from slavery to freedom, from humiliation to dignity. This is a story of redemption and new life in which the lamb gives its life to, as well as for, the people. Its blood protects and guards. Its flesh gives strength and life.

When John the Baptist called Jesus the Lamb of God, this whole story of the Passover event would have not been far from people's consciousness. As the Lamb of God, Jesus would die as the unblemished sacrifice on the cross. In John's gospel, Jesus died at precisely the same time the Passover lambs were being sacrificed in the temple.

The message is clear. The Lamb of God puts an end to the need for all further sacrifices because he has made a new and profoundly intimate relationship with God not only possible but a reality. "This is my body, which will be given up for you…. This is my blood poured out for you"—not only giving protection, not only giving physical strength, but now imparting a share in divine life itself.

That is why John the Baptist not only called Jesus the Lamb of God, but *Son* of God as well. John witnessed that announcement at Jesus's baptism himself. He knows it to be true and his testimony changed the way people saw Jesus.

Does it change the way we see him? Every week just before coming forward to receive the one who gave his life for us and to us in communion we see the elevated host and pray, "Behold the Lamb of God who takes away the sins of the world. Blessed are those called to the supper of the Lamb." Here is the one! This is the one through whom we can hope for forgiveness. This is the one who puts us in right relationship with God. This is the one who imparts the guidance of the Holy Spirit. And this is the one who actually invites us into an intimacy with God never before possible.

That ought to change the way we see everything.

The Dreamer

Isaiah 7:10–14; Romans 1:1–7; Matthew 1:18–24

"Respect your brother's dream" is a Native American proverb. How might salvation history have been changed if the sons of Jacob had honored that proverb and respected their brother Joseph's dream? We of course have no way of knowing, but we do know Joseph's story. He was Jacob's favorite son, the one with the designer multicolored coat. Joseph had dreams of his brothers bowing down to him, and when he told them about it, of course it did not go over well. Instead of respecting their brother's dream, they hatched a plot to sell him into slavery and tell their father he had been killed. Years passed. Joseph ended up in Egypt and because of his skill in interpreting dreams he saved Egypt from a famine, gained the Pharaoh's favor, rose to power, and eventually was miraculously reunited and reconciled with his brothers. (All this is found at the close of the book of Genesis, chapters 37–50.) The very next story in the Bible, the opening lines of the book of Exodus, begins many generations later when Joseph has been forgotten by the rulers of Egypt and his descendants have become slaves. Then Moses is born, narrowly escapes the Pharaoh's order that every newborn Hebrew male child be killed, and lives to lead the people to freedom.

This entire story lies just beneath the surface as Matthew begins his gospel story of a new savior of the people, Jesus of Nazareth. What better way to begin than with Joseph, the dreamer? This Joseph of Nazareth must have had his own dream. This young man about to be married must have dreamed of settling down with his wife, Mary, raising a family, maybe teaching his sons the skills of his trade. His dream would have been modest, but it would have been one of a tranquil and happy domestic existence.

But it was not to be, at least not the way he planned. Imagine how his dreams must have been shattered when he learned that Mary was pregnant and knowing he had nothing to do with it. How he must have agonized. Matthew hints at Joseph's internal struggle when he tells us Joseph reached a decision. He planned to divorce Mary quietly to spare her public shame and harm. But Joseph must have been brokenhearted.

Then he had this dream with a message from a mysterious angelic visitor that changed everything. His life was no longer his own. He would take Mary into his home as his wife, raise this child, flee to Egypt, and eventually return to Nazareth. But none of this was part of *his* dream.

It was, however, God's dream, a dream that continues to unfold even today. God's dream is to be *Emmanuel*, to share life with us. It wasn't enough for God to raise up leaders like Moses, great prophets, even kings. It wasn't enough even to send angels to intervene, reassure or even change the course of history. God desired to dwell in every human heart, to share divine life intimately with us. That could only happen by becoming human, by taking on flesh and blood and then sharing that life with us.

God's dream is realized at every Eucharist. Divine life enters human life and we are changed by it. Thank God Joseph of Nazareth laid aside his own cherished personal dream. Thank God he respected God's dream. We are indebted to him for his courage, his humility, and his faith. We are indebted to him for the gift he made possible and for the example he lived.

The Lord Is My Shepherd

Acts 2:14, 36–41; 1 Peter 2:20–25; John 10:1–10

Honestly, I don't know anything about sheep, but my neighbor Patty, who raises llamas, invited me one summer day to come over and meet two of her newest arrivals, born just weeks before. When we entered the barn every head turned, every long neck craned, and every doe eye inspected us. As the llamas recognized their owner/mama, they came over one by one to nuzzle and receive some affection. But when they spotted me it was a different story. The new mothers especially kept a wary eye on me, and their nervous bleating signaled a note of caution. It was clear they didn't trust me the way they trusted Patty. Trust, after all, has to be earned, and Patty had earned the trust of these gentle, shy creatures by caring for them: feeding, grooming, and protecting them—similar to the way a shepherd would care for sheep, I imagine.

When Jesus referred to himself as the shepherd of the sheep, he summoned a wealth of scriptural imagery in which God is seen as shepherd of the people. Psalm 23, the best known and probably most loved of all the psalms, sings eloquently of the care, comfort, protection, and guidance God the shepherd provides. This is a lasting, intimate relationship between God and the people built on trust.

Jesus has come to make that relationship even deeper and more immediate. In an ironic twist the shepherd took on the role of the sheep, the paschal lamb, to be precise, and gave his life for the flock. It is as if the shepherd said, "Over my dead body will I allow them to be harmed or lost!"

The truth is, he is not dead, but lives and now shares his own eternal, divine life with us. As Peter boldly proclaimed, we received that life at our baptism. That life is nourished at the Eucharist. It is there that the shepherd continues to care for us—feeding us from the table of the word in the Scriptures, and at the table of the altar with his own living body and blood.

Jesus has, by his authentic life, sacrificial death, and stunning resurrection earned our trust. It seems to me that all of Jesus's public ministry could be considered as one long trust-building exercise. For example:

- When Jesus invited Peter to walk on water, it went well—until Peter's trust wavered (Matthew 14:28–31).
- When a frantic father pleaded with Jesus to save his possessed son, he begged for deeper trust (Mark 9:24).
- When Jairus's daughter lay lifeless, Jesus calmly urged her father to trust since fear is useless (Mark 5:36).

Is that the key? Is it fear that keeps us from trusting the One who, according to Psalm 23, only wants "goodness and mercy" for us? Guilt, shame, punishment, judgment, and wrath all seem to be part of that fear. But where in the description of Jesus as the good shepherd is there reason to fear? And as Jesus told Philip, "Whoever sees me sees the Father" (John 14:9). So it is safe to assume the Father is also the good shepherd as Psalm 23 already proclaims. And where in that psalm is there reason to fear? In fact, Psalm 23 itself says, "Even though I walk through the valley of darkness, I fear no evil, for you are at my side with your rod and your staff to comfort me" (Psalm 23:4).

These are words of solid trust. Trust that no matter how dark the valley gets, God, the shepherd, is there. Trust that no matter how stormy the sea, God, the shepherd, is there. Trust that no matter how threatened—or threatening—life may seem, God, the shepherd, is there. Trust that no matter how final death itself may appear, God the shepherd is there.

Been there. Done that. Rose from the dead! And so will we. All we need to do is trust the shepherd. Sometimes we use another word for trust. Sometimes we call it "faith."

Sacramental Touch

1 Samuel 16:1b, 6–7, 10–13a; Ephesians 5:8–14; John 9:1–41

One Sunday morning a number of years ago when I was preaching on the gospel story of the man born blind, I have come to believe that the Holy Spirit took over and presented me and the entire congregation with a "teachable moment." I was trying to make the point of the importance we humans place on touch when this baby kept shrieking, right there, in the fourth row on the aisle, practically next to where I was standing. She wasn't an unhappy child; quite the contrary. She was very happy, but her shrieks of delight were ear-piercing and very distracting. To this day I am not sure whether it was the Holy Spirit who inspired me to ask her mom if I could hold her daughter while I continued to preach. At any rate, the mom agreed, and as I picked the little girl up in my arms I cautioned her not to shriek into the microphone. The child looked at me fascinated as I resumed trying to make the point about how important touch is to us human beings. At that point she reached out her tiny hand and started stroking my beard. I could not have made the point any better than that!

The story of the man born blind is a good illustration of sacramental touch. Just look at the story through the lens of baptism. The disciples see a problem. "Who sinned, this man or his parents?" Jesus sees a man, a human being, and a chance for God to work. The next part of the story is about as earthy as the gospels ever get. Jesus spits on the ground, makes clay, and smears it in the man's eye sockets. This is the act of creation all over again. God formed us out of clay, Genesis tells us (Genesis 2:7), and here it is as if God were to say, "Oops! Missed a spot!" This is a moment of very powerful touch. The Creator is still creating. Baptism is about the creation of new life in us.

It is comforting to remember that when Jesus encounters us in a sacrament he meets the person—not our problems, not our sinfulness. He finds in our approach a chance for God to act, to share life with us, to create again.

It is important to note that Jesus approaches us in just the same way he approached the man born blind, with profound respect. Did you notice

91

nothing happens right away after the clay is smeared on this man's eyes? And did you notice Jesus doesn't take him by the hand and lead him to the pool of Siloam? Nor does he tell Peter or anyone else to take him there. He knows this man is quite capable of navigating his world by himself and he respects this ability. He also respects his freedom. He is free to choose. He might choose not to trust, not to go, not to have faith, to remain blind. God treats us with the same respect.

In the story, the man does trust. He does believe. He does act. And when he washes in the waters of Siloam he comes to see a world he had never seen before. This is new life. It seems quite clear that John intends us to see this story as a baptism story. He calls our attention to the fact that "Siloam" means "sent." In John's gospel Jesus is the One sent into the world. He told his disciples, "My food is to do the will of *the one who sent me*" (John 4:34, emphasis added). Anyone then, washing in the baptismal waters of the pool of the one sent, is immersed in his life and in his mission.

The implications of that become clear as the man who had once been blind comes to a greater clarity of spiritual vision of just who has touched him. He grows in his understanding from "the man Jesus" to "a prophet" to a man "from God" to the "Son of Man" and finally worships Jesus as "Lord." This is quite a journey into understanding just how deeply he has been touched by God and a good demonstration of how sacraments can transform us, if we trust.

Sacraments are not magic but occasions to enter into relationship with divine mystery. Sacraments are an opportunity to allow God to reach out with a creating, healing hand to touch us, to move us, and to be with us. And as the story of the man born blind shows, that is just the beginning.

Ruby, "Man of the Year"

Hosea 6:3–6; Romans 4:18–25; Matthew 9:9–13

When I first met Father Jim he was the pastor of a small rural parish. I noticed early on that Jim had a gift for caring, especially for those the rest of us tend to overlook, ignore, or worse, look down upon. The vestibule in Jim's rectory always had numerous grocery bags stocked with food just waiting to be picked up by the next needy person to come along.

The man Jim hired to cut the grass was the village alcoholic, but in addition to paying Charlie, Jim also saw to it, through an arrangement with the local grocer, that Charlie had enough to eat, just in case Charlie drank away his pay before he bought groceries.

And then there was Ruby, the owner and manager of the village's hotel. Ruby had seen a lot in life. She spoke a rather colorful and blunt vernacular, and some would say she had rough edges to her, but she never turned away a soul in need of a meal or a bed for the night. I imagine it was that generosity toward the poor that prompted Jim to nominate her one year for the village's "Man of the Year" award. Boy, did that cause a stir! There was a virtual procession of "respectable" citizens to the rectory door imploring Jim to withdraw the nomination they viewed as embarrassing and inappropriate. Jim refused. Needless to say, Ruby was not named "Man of the Year" that year either.

But many years later, after Jim was no longer in town, he was delighted to receive an invitation to return to the village and be present at the banquet where Ruby would receive the newly retooled "Person of the Year" award.

It must have given Jim great satisfaction to join in that banquet where Ruby took her place of honor among the leading citizens of the village. Some of that satisfaction undoubtedly would have come from the fact that the scene where he sat so well reflected the gospel where Jesus welcomed everyone to his table, *everyone*. He seemed to go out of his way to invite those one would have expected to be excluded.

Tax collectors, like Matthew, in general were not beloved by the people.

And sinners were, well—not exactly paradigms of virtue. One avoided the bad influences of either of these groups.

So why did Jesus include these individuals any "respectable" citizen would have excluded? That was the question asked of Jesus's disciples who must have felt uncomfortable and embarrassed themselves. Evidently the question was asked none too subtly since Jesus himself overheard it. His response: these are the people who needed him. How could he turn them away?

But there is another answer here as well, one expressed not in words but in action. The table in Jesus's own home is a living parable of the banquet of heaven where all are welcomed with open arms regardless of social status, character flaws, personal mistakes, or basic human weaknesses.

One of the prayers at our own Eucharist calls our gathering here "the foretaste and the promise of the paschal feast of heaven" So our gathering at the Eucharist then is, like the table in Jesus's own home in the gospel, a sign of the banquet of heaven. When we gather at the Lord's table we are welcomed with open arms without regard to social status, character flaws, personal mistakes, or human weaknesses.

What a comfort that is. As we look around the table we see our common humanity. We are each made in the image and likeness of God. We all come from the same divine Creator and so are in fact brothers and sisters. That is not metaphor. It is the lesson Jesus lived every day. It is the lesson he drew very pointedly in the gospel, and it is a lesson Father Jim taught me many years ago as he welcomed the poor stranger at his door looking for food, supported Charlie, who was struggling with alcoholism—and nominated Ruby to be "Man of the Year."

Some Seed Fell on Good Ground

Isaiah 55:10–11; Romans 8:18–23; Matthew 13:1–9

Late one summer my neighbor Roger planted the sixty-four acres that surround my home with winter wheat. By fall the wheat had sprouted, creating a rolling carpet of green. Then in late winter and early spring the rains came, melting the ice and snow that had blanketed the fields producing so much water it created a small lake. The water was deep enough that the returning geese could not only wade in it but swim. I even joked that suddenly I lived on waterfront property. It took several months for all that water to finally drain away, leaving behind a big patch of mud flats. That following summer there were nothing but weeds growing in that temporary lakebed, but it was surrounded by a field of ripening winter wheat.

It was as if the parable Jesus told in the gospel about the sower was growing right outside my door. Of course, the parable has nothing to do with sound agricultural practices. Jesus was interested in something more profound and more lasting than that. When Jesus began, "A sower went out to sow," he told a story that has become so familiar to us that anyone could tell it by heart. It is a parable that reveals the nature of the kingdom of a generous, even prodigal God who casts out seeds everywhere, even where their prospects for success are not very promising. In that respect it reflects Jesus's own ministry preaching, teaching, and inviting the rich as well as the poor, the wise as well as the simple, and the powerful as well as the powerless.

As the gospel continues, Jesus explains the parable. The seeds represent God's word. We are so used to this story that it may not impress us much, especially in a world where we are drowning in words from every side: radio, TV, computers, phones that seem to be everywhere, and even those maddening disclaimers at the end of radio ads that speak at a pace faster than is humanly possible to understand.

But consider for a moment what your word is when you are conversing with another person. Isn't it at least in some way an extension of yourself? Isn't it a way to influence or touch another? Isn't it a way of reaching out? That is what God's Word is. The Word that not only reached out but created the other, and as Isaiah so confidently pointed out, God's Word still contains that life-kindling power. How appropriate that Jesus compared God's Word to a seed, and even more appropriate when you realize Jesus is God's Word in flesh and blood.

The sower and the seed represent God's action in this parable, but what about our side? What kind of reception do we give God's Word? What kind of soil are we?

"Some seed fell on the path and birds came and ate it up." Jesus explains this represents one who hears the Word, does not understand it, and then the evil one comes and snatches it away. It saddens me when I have conversations with those who say they used to be Catholic but aren't anymore. Then as the conversation continues it becomes apparent that they never understood their own faith in the first place: what Jesus is about, what the Scriptures really say, what the sacraments really mean, and what we do at the Eucharist.

"Some seed fell on rocky soil. It sprouted but then the sun came up and scorched it." Jesus explains these are the people who receive the Word with great enthusiasm and then lose interest. We live in a whole world like that. New Years' resolutions that don't make it to February, Lenten resolutions that might survive to the second Sunday of Lent, great intentions that never seem to translate into actions.

"Some seed fell among thorns." There are so many suffocating dangers out there especially in our culture always inviting us to consume more, want more, get more. There seems to be an ever-expanding list of addictions to which we are vulnerable.

But then there is the fertile soil. There is hope. We can listen to the Word, the Scriptures, as well as the whisperings of the Spirit in our own hearts. We can embrace the Word and we can respond. God has generously cast the seed; we can support its growth within us.

That little lakebed of weeds by my house was dwarfed to insignificance by the golden wheat stretching for acres around it. And later that summer the town installed a brand new drainage system, which will probably keep the parable from repeating itself.

It also goes to show we have it in our power to improve our own soil.

A Field of Daisies

The Wisdom of Solomon 12; 13, 16–19;
Romans 8:26–27; Matthew 13:24–30

Newell had farmed his land for decades. One year he needed to borrow a piece of equipment from a neighboring farmer to harvest one of his fields. He never thought much about it until late the following spring when that same field became a sea of daisies. There had never been any daisies there before, but Newell figured that the equipment he had borrowed must have been loaded with daisy seeds. It took years to get rid of those tenacious weeds (Newell used a more colorful adjective to describe them), but eventually it was rendered daisy-free and yielded healthy crops.

Of course, the "daisy contamination" was completely accidental and unintentional, unlike the crop contamination in the parable Jesus told describing the kingdom of heaven. In his parable the enemy sows weeds throughout the field with malicious intentions, but what is striking about this parable is how the landowner handles the situation. He does not try to retaliate against the enemy, which is what one would have expected in that situation. He allows the weeds to continue to grow along with the wheat. As he wisely points out, trying to prematurely pull the weeds might do more harm than good, destroying some of the wheat. At harvest time he ends up having the last laugh on his enemy since he now not only has wheat in his barn but fuel all bundled up and ready to burn.

What does this tell us about the kingdom of heaven? For one thing there seem to be two phases to the kingdom, or perhaps two dimensions. One is the present time represented in the parable by the growing season, and the other is the future, represented by the harvest. In the present the wheat and weeds are growing together. There is a mixture of good and bad in our world. We don't have to look too far to verify that. But before we too easily divide our world into good people and bad people, perhaps the parable is saying there is a mixture of good and bad in each of us. That's a rather sobering thought that makes this parable hit closer to home than perhaps we are comfortable with. But that's what parables do.

This parable also seems to say that while there will always be a mixture of good and bad in our world we need to be patient, with ourselves and with our less-than-perfect world. There is good reason for this patience. It all rests in God's hands anyway. That is the nature of the kingdom of heaven: it is what God does. The kingdom is not some particular place, not some government, not some organization, not even the church. The kingdom of heaven is simply what God does with or without our cooperation, as Father Thomas Keating points out on page108 in his book *The Mystery of Christ*.

And what God does ensures that the wheat is strong enough to not only survive the weeds but to bear fruit. In addition to all this the image of the seed should not be overlooked or underestimated. It starts small but bears fruit. Good will win out eventually in ourselves and in our world. That may be hard to believe in the present moment, but maybe we are not looking in the right places, or through the proper lens.

A few years ago in Buffalo, New York Sister Karen Klimczak, a nun who had devoted her life to working with ex-cons at a halfway house was murdered by a resident. In a crowded courtroom as her convicted killer was about to be sentenced Sister Karen's sister read aloud a letter written fifteen years before by Sister Karen, somehow anticipating and at the same time forgiving her murderer. In the letter Sister Karen wrote, "Dear Brother, I don't know what the circumstances are that will lead you to hurt me or destroy my physical body... No, I don't want it to happen. I would much rather enjoy the beauties of this earth, experience the laughter, the fears and the tears of those I love so deeply! Now my life has changed and you, my brother, were the instrument of that change. I forgive you for what you have done and I will always watch over you, help you in whatever way I can... Continue living always mindful of His presence, His love and His joy as sources of life itself — then my life will have been worth being changed through you." Today, Sister Karen Klimczak's life inspires and her work continues at that halfway house.

A social worker was absolutely stunned to learn from her clients that food stamps do not cover diapers. They seem to be considered a luxury, like alcohol and tobacco. As a result some children wear the same diaper way too long and some cannot be admitted to daycare because the parents cannot provide the required extra diapers. So she started a diaper drive and today is distributing thousands of diapers every week. (Her program has no name yet, but one wit suggested "No Child Wet Behind.")

During his final days in the hospital a man from my parish asked that the small lap robe parishioners had made for him be brought to him. He felt it brought him closer to the community. I don't think it would be stretching it to say Pete died in their loving embrace. That's what the kingdom of heaven is like.

Keys

Isaiah 22:19–23; Romans 11:33–36; Matthew 16:13–20

Many years ago in Rome, American students studying for the priesthood lived in a neighborhood where the very narrow streets were paved with cobblestones. Sound traveled easily there, especially in the relative stillness of a Roman evening.

It so happened that every night a young man would appear in the street just below a window immediately opposite the seminary and in a plaintiff voice call out to his girlfriend. Soon she would appear at the window and toss down a key that would loudly tinkle on the cobblestones. The young man would then scramble to snatch it up and quickly disappear into the building. This little ritual went on practically every night.

So one day the seminarians took up a collection in the house of every key they could find that no longer served any useful purpose. They nearly filled a cigar box with old keys. That night when the unsuspecting young man arrived in the street below, the seminarians were ready. Just when the young lady tossed her key out her window, from the window on the opposite side of the street a whole torrent of keys of every size and shape rained down on the unfortunate young man in the street below. For all I know he is still looking for the right key.

Keys are very much a part of our lives. How many keys do you have in your pocket or purse right now? Keys open doors to our homes, to cars, to safe deposit boxes, to treasured thoughts locked away in secret diaries, and to so many other places in our lives. But how do we see the "keys to the kingdom of heaven" that Jesus entrusted to Peter?

In popular mythology Peter stands at the pearly gates of heaven firmly set in celestial clouds admitting or denying entry to each soul who presents itself before him. Is that really what Jesus had in mind? Did Jesus imply that Peter would wield a kind of earthly power imposed on his subjects similar to the power exercised by other rulers and autocrats of the world?

Neither of these scenarios seems adequate when we consider that Jesus made his promise to give Peter the keys to the kingdom of heaven right on the heels of Peter's astounding profession of faith in Jesus as "the Christ, the son of the living God."

These keys are different. Keys provide access. Keys open the way. These keys entrusted to Peter are meant to provide access to God here and now. And that is how the gospel speaks to us today. It isn't just Peter who was entrusted with the keys but the whole community of faith that will follow after him right down to the present moment. In the same breath that Jesus calls Peter "the rock" and promises him the keys, he also says he will build his church, which is the entire community of believers, on that "rock." So we, the church, have inherited Peter's promise, and our community of faith still holds the keys to the kingdom of heaven.

It is important to note that these keys are not about lording it over others. They are not about excluding others or locking anyone out. These keys open the way and include others, just as Jesus opened the way for others and included them.

The church may have been entrusted with the keys to the kingdom, but the church is not the kingdom. It is far too human for that! So just what might these keys be? Perhaps our shared faith in the risen Christ. Maybe the sacraments, each one a precious key that leads us, in its own way, into a deep encounter with God and a heightened awareness of our deep connection with each other. Or perhaps it's our tradition of prayer and the numerous ways our traditions, devotions, and piety bring us closer to God and each other.

Maybe there are other keys you might identify for yourself as meaningful keys to the kingdom of heaven. It would seem Jesus did not give Peter, and us, just a single key like the one that young man sought night after night in Rome many years ago. No, it was a whole torrent of keys—each opening the way to Divine encounter.

Those Pesky Parables

Isaiah 5:1–7; Philippians 4:6–9; Matthew 21:33–43

Parables are comparisons. Parables are challenges. And parables are questions always directed at the listener. Matthew's fingerprints are all over this parable of the vineyard in the form it has come down to us. Matthew probably embellished Jesus's original parable drawn from Isaiah's song of the vineyard and then adapted it to his own time. The principle elements are not difficult to identify: the vineyard is Israel; the tenants are Israel's leaders; the vineyard owner is God; the various messengers are the prophets; and the son, of course, is Jesus.

The parable unfolds in a tragic but familiar pattern. God has showered Israel with blessings: freedom from slavery, a homeland of their own, their own identity, and a special (covenantal) relationship with him; but how is that repaid? It would appear with total indifference for God and their relationship to him.

But God does not give up. In an effort to draw Israel back to himself, prophet after prophet is sent to the people, but this doesn't go well either. The prophets did not have an easy time of it, to say the least. At one point things go so bad that the great prophet Elijah lays down in the wilderness and prays for death. Jeremiah was beaten, ridiculed, and thrown down a cistern where he sank into the mud, and Amos was told to shut up and go back where he came from. Being a prophet was not an easy career path.

In one last desperate attempt God sends his Son. In the parable the son is thrown outside the vineyard and murdered, a clear reference to how Jesus actually died. He was arrested, dragged outside the city of Jerusalem, and crucified, his ultimate rejection by the established Jewish leaders.

The parable is certainly an indictment of that crowd, but the parable does not end there. Just who are the "other tenants" to whom God entrusts the vineyard at the end of the parable? Because of the times and circumstances in which Matthew's gospel was written, in all likelihood they must be the leaders of the Jewish Christian community. When Matthew's gospel was being written there was a growing tension between the Jewish community who followed Jesus and the Jewish community who did not. It wouldn't be long before the two would part ways and Christianity would follow its own path.

Now while all this may be helpful historical information to better understand where we came from, what does this gospel have to say to us today?

Parables are comparisons. Parables are challenges. Parables are questions always directed at the listener and we happen to be the listeners here. So this parable is also acting as a mirror, inviting us to deeper reflection.

What is the vineyard in our lives? It might represent all the blessings God has given us. In a way the vineyard is not so different from the garden of Eden. And the storyline is about the same. What blessings do we enjoy? Freedom, faith, family, friendship, community, and companionship, just for starters. But how do we respond to God? Are we indifferent? In other words, do we respond with greed rather than gratitude? Greed is so pervasive in our culture we may have absorbed some of it without even knowing. Apparently it was greed on a massive scale that got us into this terrible economic situation we find ourselves facing these days. How much have we "bought into" it? Even our language betrays us.

And here is another consideration. The tenants in the vineyard were hostile to anyone sent to hold them accountable or challenge them. How do we respond to those who would challenge us in any way? In what ways might we actually be beating up on each other? Remember what Jesus said in chapter 25 in Matthew's gospel, that whatever we do to each other we do to him. Is it possible we might be throwing the Son out of the vineyard without even knowing it?

The tenants in the parable want power. Jesus demonstrated to his disciples that real power comes through service to each other. The tenants in the parable want wealth, but Jesus reveals that true wealth can only be found by giving one's self away.

On deeper consideration, perhaps the tenants in that parable are not so different from us as we may have thought. That is an unsettling thought and it is a challenge; again, that's what parables are supposed to do. But there is also a consolation with this parable—in fact, with all parables. And it is this: Jesus would never have bothered to tell this parable or any other parable if it did not also contain the seeds of hope that maybe this time someone will listen.

Standing on the Threshold

Isaiah 42:1–4, 6–7; Acts 10:34–38; Matthew 3:13–17

It was a beautiful September evening in 1975 as I stood in the doorway of Our Mother of Sorrows church. The faithful had assembled and were waiting for Mass to begin. For me this Eucharist would be a life-changing event because it was the night I would be ordained a priest. The road leading to this moment had been long and not without its own twists, turns, and surprises. As I stood there next to Bishop Hogan feeling many different emotions simultaneously, I realized I was literally standing at a threshold. Once I passed through that doorway, life would never be the same. It was exciting. It was joyful. It was humbling, and it was a little scary. Threshold moments are like that. Just ask any bride or groom.

We cannot even begin to imagine the thoughts and emotions Jesus must have felt on the banks of the Jordan River as he stood on a threshold that would forever alter not only his life but ours. Once Jesus passed through the waters of John's baptism, his public ministry would begin.

The people submitting to John's baptism sought forgiveness for their sins and committed themselves to a whole new way of life. But Jesus didn't need forgiveness, so why did he insist on being baptized? This moment signaled a whole new life for Jesus and perhaps baptism would not only ritualize that beginning but maybe even help to clarify it. That seems to be what Jesus meant by his rather mystifying response to John, "Allow it for now. For thus it is fitting for us to fulfill all righteousness" (Matthew 3:15).

And so Jesus was immersed in the waters of the Jordan, the waters in which human sinfulness had been ritually washed away. But rather than having sins washed away he took on the human condition. Jesus immersed himself in our sinfulness, our faults, and our weakness. And when he rose up out of the waters he carried us with him all the way to the end. Perhaps the mission itself became clearer to him even as he came up out of the river. Jesus himself may have come to John with an undefined purpose. Maybe he even wondered deep within, "Who am I? And what does God want from me?" Two very human questions.

For Jesus the answer came quickly. "After Jesus was baptized, he came up from the water and behold, the heavens were opened for him, and he saw the Spirit of God descending like a dove and coming upon him. And a voice came from heaven saying, 'This is my beloved Son, with whom I am well pleased'" (Matthew 3:16–17). It all points to who Jesus is.

That the heavens were opened tells us there is a new channel of communication between heaven and earth, between God and humanity. Now real communion is possible. "My Son" indicates Jesus as heir to King David and entitled to be called Son of God (Psalm 2:7). "Beloved" recalls Isaac, Abraham's beloved son, who carried the wood of his own sacrifice up the mountain (Genesis 22:2, 6). "With whom I am well pleased" recalls the servant of God from Isaiah who brings light, justice and compassion.

All these things manifest who Jesus is, but what do they really mean for us? Could it be that his experience might be found in our own experience? After all, Jesus is fully human just like us. What power drew him to this moment in his life? What compelled him to leave a nice quiet life in Galilee to begin this very demanding and dangerous public ministry? Why did he leave the comforts of home to wander all over Palestine preaching, teaching, healing, arguing, sacrificing, and ultimately dying?

Could it have been "the voice"? In the rabbinic tradition a voice from heaven is known as the *bat qol*, the daughter of the voice or the echo of a word uttered in heaven.

It is a compelling voice and I suspect we all have heard it at one time or another. Oh, not from the heavens but from deep within, from the very core of who we are. At times it might just be that nagging question: "Who am I and what does God want from me?"

We can try to ignore or even resist it especially when it seems to point us in a direction we would rather not go, but I can assure you of this, the voice cannot ever be denied. It will hound you because it springs from the deepest part of you.

"I, the Lord, have called you" (Isaiah 42:6) Isaiah says, indicating the ultimate source of "the voice" and why we call it a *vocation*.

Christmas

Isaiah 9:1–6; Titus 2:11–14; Luke 2:1–14

I grew up in St. Margaret Mary's parish in Irondequoit, New York, and every year at Christmas the statue of St. Margaret Mary would disappear from its niche. In its stead appeared a thick fragrant evergreen forest. In the center of this wood was a stable lined with straw and the familiar scene of Mary, Joseph, and the infant Jesus flanked by shepherds and sheep. The magi came later. It was magical. The story is magical. All of us know it so well we can retell it with every cherished detail. I know of no other story that can motivate us to recreate it not only in our churches but in our homes as well.

Every figure in it, every detail, contains a depth we may not be aware of but we feel on some level.

Mary and Joseph have come a long way. Each has been visited by an angel so they know God is with them, but God has been frustratingly skimpy on the details. So here they are in Bethlehem without a place to stay and the baby is coming tonight. Talk about trust! And why Bethlehem? We are told it is because of a census requirement, but more importantly it is because Bethlehem is "the city of David," the great king whose descendant will come to rule again as king. This baby is a descendant of David. He will be known as Christ the king.

"There were shepherds in the region, living in the fields and keeping watch by night over their flocks" (Luke 2:8). Shepherds were not always held in high esteem, living away from home and sometimes suspected of lifting whatever wasn't nailed down. On the other hand, David was a shepherd right there in Bethlehem. David was king, shepherd, and capable leader. Unfortunately, his successors often were not. The prophet Ezekiel leveled this scathing criticism against the shepherd-kings of Israel, saying "you do not feed the sheep. You have not strengthened the weak, you have not healed the sick, you have not bound up the injured, you have not brought back the strayed, you have not sought the lost" (Ezekiel 34:3–4). To correct the situation the prophet continues, "For thus says the Lord God: I myself will search for my sheep … and I will feed them with good pasture" (Ezekiel 34:11, 14).

God keeps his promises, and when this baby grew to manhood did he not refer to himself as the Good Shepherd? He is the one who strengthens the weak, heals the sick, binds up the injured, brings back the strayed, and seeks out the lost. The sheep are once again cared for and cared about. The shepherds who came to his side that night recognized the Good Shepherd and represented Israel coming home.

Do you have an ox and a donkey in your manger scene at home? They are not just a couple of quaint or accidental animals here. The book of Isaiah opens with the lines "The ox knows its owner and the donkey its master's crib, but Israel does not know and my people do not understand" (Isaiah 1:3).

The angels tie earth to heaven as they always have since walking with Abraham (Genesis 18:2) and going up and down the ladder Jacob dreamed of at Bethel (Genesis 28:12).

But it is the manger itself that offers the most profound reflection. For here on this bed of straw resting in the feeding place for animals lies the bread of life. When this child grew to manhood he would announce, "I am the bread of life ... whoever eats this bread will live forever" (John 6:48, 51). This is the bread from heaven that feeds us and shares divine life with us. Tonight, Earth is indeed united to heaven and divine life enters human life, transforming us and leading us home.

We are the sheep and the Good Shepherd has come.

We're Expecting

Isaiah 63:16b–17, 19b, 64:2b–7; 1 Corinthians 1:3–9; Mark 13:33–37

One evening in early September more than forty years ago, I had just enjoyed a fine pot roast dinner that Pat, my very pregnant sister-in-law, had prepared. We cleared the table and washed the dishes and were about to go into the living room to relax a bit when Pat disappeared for a few minutes. When she returned she announced that the baby was on its way. All I remember from that point on was a single-minded dedication to get this soon-to-be-mom to the hospital—pronto! For weeks Pat had been unable to ride comfortably in a car because of her condition. She needed to sit higher and have more room. Fortunately the cab in my brother's truck was just right. But the truck needed a driver, and for reasons not critical to the story I ended up being the designated driver. I can assure you that all the way to the hospital I felt like I was channeling both Mario Andretti and an EMT. Believe me, I was focused. To quote the famous line from *Gone With the Wind*, "I don't know nothin' 'bout birthin' babies!"

Fortunately, we arrived at the hospital in plenty of time. Pat was promptly admitted and whisked away, and several hours later my nephew, Mike, was born—appropriately on Labor Day. (After the Mass where I had told this story, a very pregnant parishioner walked by and said, "I'm going home and making a pot roast!")

Excitement, anticipation, joy, waiting, and patience are just a few words that describe both the birth of a child and the season of Advent. Yet all too often, I am afraid, we have heard Jesus's command to "Watch!" more as an ominous threat than as the promise of imminent new life, which it is.

Jesus came, Mark will tell us repeatedly, to announce the kingdom of God breaking into human history. Like the birth of a child there is a suddenness about it, an urgency, but not dread. This coming of the kingdom is something that has been longed for over the ages. Isaiah prayed with great earnestness, "Lord, Father, our Redeemer … oh that you would rend the heavens and come down!" Be with us! Restore our lives! Give us hope! This is not dread.

It is a prayer that is answered when Jesus does come. Mark's gospel makes no mention at all of the circumstances surrounding Jesus's birth, but at his baptism Mark depicts a scene that vividly evokes Isaiah's prayer. As Jesus comes up out of the waters of his own baptism, Mark says, "He saw the heavens being torn open and the Spirit, like a dove, descending upon him" (Mark 1:10).

Jesus came to announce the kingdom, and we look for him to come again to bring the fullness of the kingdom where there will be no more suffering, injustice, division, pain, violence, or death. The liturgical focus of the early days of Advent are on that second coming of Christ and the fullness of the kingdom, eternal happiness, peace, and fulfillment. Why should we dread that as we watch and wait? Do expectant parents dread the approaching birth of a child?

Babies have a way of changing their parents' lives even before they arrive. There is so much to do. Set up the nursery, stock up on all kinds of baby needs—crib, blankets, diapers, PJs, bottles—the list goes on and on. There may even be adjustments in routines. But it is all done with a certain sense of excitement and anticipation because a new life is about to be welcomed into the world. There is a focus.

Advent is like that. All the stuff we need to do. All the errands we have to run. All the baking that has to happen and cards that have to be written and sent. All the gifts we need to find, make, wrap, and exchange can be distractions from the meaning of the season, if we allow them to be. On the other hand, all these activities can become moments of preparation and even encounter with the Lord present already if we stay focused on who it is we honor by doing all these things.

It's like the overworked innkeeper in Bethlehem two thousand years ago, frantically trying to provide for all the guests in a full house and there's a knock on the door. Little did he know that in the middle of all his frenzied activity—in his efforts to creatively provide for this homeless and desperate young couple—he was providing the setting for Isaiah's prayer to finally be answered: "Oh, that you would rend the heavens and come down!"

What Did You Expect to See?

Isaiah 61:1–2a, 10–11; 1 Thessalonians 5:16–24; John 1:6–8, 19–28

He hardly looked or sounded like John the Baptist. In fact, the contrast is stunning. He was—well, let's just say "not thin." He was soft spoken, rather quiet, humble, unassuming, and deeply reflective. His name was Father Benjamin Willaert and he taught systematic theology at the University of Louvain, Belgium. Some of his students had affectionately and appropriately nicknamed him "Gentle Ben."

He used to arrive at class, open his notes on the desk in the front of the room, and then ignore them for the rest of the period. With one hand in the side pocket of his suit jacket and the index finger of his other hand thoughtfully poised on his lips he would pace back and forth, posing knotty theological questions and struggling with the problems they presented. It drove the type-A personalities in the class crazy. They wanted a nice neat package with headings, indents, and answers. But then there were the others like myself who were fascinated at witnessing the very process of what theology is all about: *fides quaerens intellectum,* as St. Thomas Aquinas expressed it—"faith seeking understanding." In nearly every class Father Willaert would start with one question and by the end of class would arrive not at an answer, but at a different, more profound question.

Theologians are sometimes maligned for being too abstract, academic, and divorced from the "real world." But with Ben Willaert one had the sense this theologian was reflecting not on some abstraction but on the core of the meaning of life and his own faith. Although he never spoke of it in personal terms, you just knew he had a deep, abiding faith. That he, like Jacob in the Old Testament, had wrestled with the angel (Genesis 32:23–31). And he had emerged from the struggle with a rock-solid faith, a sense of trust even when you do not have the answers to life's questions. Ben Willaert not only instructed his students, he inspired them. He pointed to the light among us just as John the Baptist testified to the "one among you whom you do not recognize."

Is that still true today? Could God be present among us and we still do not recognize him? At the Last Judgment scene in Matthew's gospel, the King says to the just, "I was hungry and you gave me food, I was thirsty and you gave me drink, a stranger and you welcomed me, naked and you clothed me, ill and you cared for me, in prison and you visited me" (Matthew 25:35–36). It would seem that it is altogether possible Christ is present and we do not recognize him. And it would follow that we still need the mission of John the Baptist to testify to divine presence among us that we may be overlooking.

So who has been John the Baptist for you? Who has pointed to Christ's presence for you? She or he may not come quickly to mind and you may have to sit with that question for a while. She or he may be the most unassuming, humble, ordinary person. They may not stand out in any way at all. I think it safe to say whoever it may be was not clothed in camel's hair and munching on locusts and honey.

Maybe your John the Baptist is a family member, a teacher, a friend, or a neighbor, maybe all of the above. Whoever it is, something about this person pointed beyond himself or herself. Could it be that maybe *you* have been John the Baptist for someone else?

The Paradox of Power

The Wisdom of Solomon 2:12, 17–20; James 3:16, 4:3; Mark 9:30–37

At the beginning of his public ministry, just after being baptized by John, all three synoptic gospels (Matthew, Mark, and Luke) tell us Jesus went into the desert for forty days where he was tested by the Devil. During one of these temptations the Devil took Jesus up on to a high mountain, showed him all the kingdoms of the world, with their wealth, power, and glory, and offered, "All these I shall give you if you will prostrate yourself and worship me" (Matthew 4:9).

What a deal! Who wouldn't want power and control in their life? I'll bet there are at least a few people in your life you'd like to tell what to do, where to go, and how to get there. Sounds attractive, doesn't it? But it's a dead end. It's a dead end because at its heart it is self-centered, and self-centeredness keeps us from entering into relationship with God and one another. And it is in those relationships that we become truly and deeply human.

Jesus rejected the temptation outright, recognizing it for what it is: a road to disillusionment and a recipe for frustration. If you start grasping for power, do you ever feel you have enough? That's the road the disciples were on. Jesus had begun his journey to Jerusalem and the cross, but his disciples had chosen another route. All along the way they argued about who was going to get the power, the status, the rank. When they got home and inside the house, Jesus asked them, perhaps like a disappointed parent, "What were you arguing about along the way?" The question really wasn't necessary. In that culture nobody whispered. Jesus had heard. He probably just wanted them to look at themselves fighting over power, a power they assumed was coming their way, a power they expected to share, to wield, and to enjoy.

Nobody wanted to think about what Jesus had just told them for the second time—that he was going to die. And they certainly didn't understand the part about "rising again." So they ignored it. "I don't know. I don't want to know. Don't tell me about it. I'll worry." There are many who have traveled the difficult road to recovery from addiction who will tell you, "Denial is not just a river in Egypt."

To face down this denial Jesus sat down, taking the posture of a teacher. He flatly told his disciples if they really wanted to be first, they had to be the last—and the least. Power was out of the question. Taking a child, Jesus wrapped his arms around her, looked up at these grown men, and made them notice her. This may not sound like much, but in Jesus's time and culture, children were virtually invisible. They were inconsequential little nobodies with about the same status as a slave until they reached adulthood, if they reached adulthood. Thirty percent of children died before they reached age six, and another 60 percent died before reaching the teen years. To be a child was to be vulnerable, powerless, and voiceless, and it is in just such persons Jesus told his disciples (and us) that he and the One who sent him can be found.

That leaves us with the following questions: Who might be the vulnerable, powerless, voiceless, and maybe even despised in our time and place? Are they, like the children in Jesus's day, virtually invisible? Do we even notice them?

At St. Joseph's House of Hospitality in Rochester, New York, a Catholic worker center, at one time on a certain day of the week any homeless person who showed up at their door not only received food for the day but was actually invited to take a seat while one of their volunteers removed his or her shoes and socks, bathed and dried the person's feet, and put a new pair of socks on for him or her.

"Whoever receives one such as this receives me. And whoever receives me receives not me but the One who sent me" (Mark 9:37).

Lost and Found

Exodus 32:7–14; 1 Timothy 1:12–17; Luke 15:1–32

When I was growing up, our family pet was a German shorthaired pointer named Skipper. He was, like most pets, part of the family. Skip was a fast runner, full of energy, and swimming was his specialty. One winter morning we woke to discover the disturbing fact that Skip had managed to get out of his kennel and was nowhere to be found. We searched frantically for him all over the neighborhood, but no one had seen him. The search stretched out all day and still no luck. We began to lose hope of ever seeing him again. As evening came the family had to go away for a while; I can't remember why. I just remember that as soon as we got home again I went out to Skipper's kennel hoping against hope he would be there. I called his name, but there was no response, just stillness. I turned and started back toward the house trudging through the snow and very depressed, when suddenly from behind Skipper came trotting happily along to greet me. That it was a happy reunion would be a gross understatement. That night Skipper got the royal treatment. We were all so happy to have him back home—like the shepherd who found his lost sheep, the woman her lost coin, and the father his wayward son.

Jesus often drew from the life experiences of his audience to reveal God present in their lives. In three deceptively simple parables strung together like pearls, Jesus reveals a God passionately seeking us out like a shepherd traipsing through the wilderness in search of one stray sheep. What a relief when he finds it. He doesn't even grumble as he hoists it up onto his shoulders and brings it home. In fact, he couldn't be happier. God carries us on his shoulders and is happy to do it. Do you ever think of God that way? Yet here it is right in front of us.

And what about the woman scouring every inch of her home looking for that evasive coin? Using lamplight she examines every nook and cranny, knowing it has to be there somewhere. And then when she does find it—she throws a party to celebrate! Here is one of those often overlooked feminine images of God. Do you ever think of her that way? Yet here she is right from Jesus himself. Perhaps she deserves more attention than we usually give her.

The father of the prodigal son must have scanned the distant horizon every day looking for his son because in the parable "while he was still a long way off his father caught sight of him and was filled with compassion. He ran to his son, embraced him, and kissed him." God is not only filled with compassion for us but he runs to us, embraces us, and even kisses us! Do you ever think of God that way?

But there is still one more image that tells us just how deeply beloved by God we are—the fatted calf. The father could have ordered a lamb, sheep, or goat to be prepared, but the calf is a feast for a hundred people. This is a feast for the entire community. Everyone is included.

Remember the complaint of the Pharisees and scribes that prompted these parables, "This man welcomes sinners and eats with them." At the table Jesus provides everyone is welcome and everyone is invited. We call it Eucharist. This is a grand banquet for the entire community provided by the One who carries us on his shoulders, searches for us in every nook and cranny and runs to embrace us in infinite compassion and mercy. And all this time we thought *we* were looking for God.

The Lamb of God

Isaiah 49:3–6; 1 Corinthians 1:1–3; John 1:29–34

If you have ever attended the Easter Vigil celebration you know it always begins with the blessing of the new fire kindled out in front of the church. The new paschal candle is lit from the fire and we all process into the dark church where each person soon holds a lighted candle, bathing the entire church in soft light.

Father Tom Reddington loved that liturgy and he used to see to it at the Easter Vigil that his Weber grill was placed in the walled courtyard of his parish church of the Holy Name of Jesus with an impressive fire blazing away, its flames leaping high up and visible to all inside through the glass wall of the church as the vigil began. After a few hours, as the Easter Vigil ended, the roaring fire would have become a bed of red hot coals, just right for barbecuing.

So after the parishioners went home Tom would wheel the grill around behind the rectory, put the grate back in place, and then, over the coals, put the butterflied lamb that had been marinating all day. A short time later Tom would preside at table over an Easter feast with a few close friends enjoying that lamb roasted on the paschal fire.

The significance of that meal was not lost on those of us who were privileged to share in it. Tom was, in a way, extending the liturgy by recalling the Passover meal itself with roasted lamb, the meal of the Israelites as they prepared to escape Egypt, slavery, and a life without hope.

It was the tradition of that Passover lamb that John called to mind when he identified Jesus as the "Lamb of God," a title that would sound strange to us if it were not so familiar. Every Eucharist we ourselves repeat it three times just before communion: "Lamb of God, who take away the sins of the world, have mercy on us. Lamb of God, who take away the sins of the world, have mercy on us. Lamb of God, who take away the sins of the world, grant us peace." Then once more we hear the words of John the Baptist himself, "Behold the Lamb of God, who takes away the sins of the world."

In John's gospel Jesus *is* the Passover lamb. The Exodus story tells how the unblemished lamb was slaughtered, its blood splashed on the doorposts of the Israelites, protecting them from the death that was befalling the Egyptians. The lamb's flesh was roasted and eaten as food for their journey. The lamb's blood saved and protected the people while its roasted flesh gave them the strength they needed for their journey to freedom.

The gospels draw a striking parallel between Jesus and the Passover lamb. At Mass we recall the night before he died Jesus took bread, broke it, and gave it to his friends, saying, "Take this and eat it. This is my body, given up for you." Then he took the cup and said, "This is the cup of my blood. It will be shed for you and for all so that sins may be forgiven." Like the paschal lamb Jesus's body becomes food for our life. His blood protects and saves. Of course it doesn't end there. Jesus is the Lamb of God, alive and in us and among us. His flesh becomes our flesh and we share his life. His blood courses through our veins with its saving power. On Easter Sunday afternoon he gave us even more—his breath, the Holy Spirit. And so we breathe with the power of the Holy Spirit.

Now here's the challenge. Just as it was up to Israel to respond to God's saving action, leading them to freedom, so it is our challenge to live the life that has been given to us.

A number of years ago when the spring thaw had really begun to take hold, all the streams and creeks around the Buffalo area became, as they always do in this season, raging muddy torrents of water overflowing their banks and rushing along with great force. One young man, a high school student, whose backyard bordered one of these streams, got the idea that he would cross the now-raging waters on a log that lay across the stream. He had probably done just that hundreds of times before when the stream was much more tranquil. But this time he slipped off the log, was swept away in the water, and drowned. I can still hear the voice of his grieving mother in a burst of raw maternal honesty say, "I am so angry with my son for not treating the life I gave him with more respect and care."

How well do we live the life that has been given to us? Life that would rather serve than be served, life that would bring true peace to the world through compassion, tolerance and forgiveness, life that is marked by generosity and self-sacrifice.

117

When we receive the Lamb of God in the Eucharist, we receive the One who gave himself for others and now challenges us to do the same. With that realization, could we ever approach the Lamb of God in communion with anything but the deepest respect, reverence, and gratitude?

It's Your Fault!

Genesis 2:7–9, 3:1–7; Romans 5:12–19; Matthew 4:1–11

I must have been around seven or eight years old when Mom and Dad left me and my older brother home alone for a few hours one afternoon. Frankly, I don't remember how it all started, but somehow the two of us got to roughhousing as brothers often do. He was chasing me all over the house. I was always faster. At one point we ended up at opposite ends of the living room. Behind me at my end of the room were some built-in bookcases with glass doors. At the other end of the room was a very frustrated older brother who had not been able to catch me. So he took off one of his shoes (do I need to even finish this?) and winged it at me. Of course I ducked and then heard that undeniable sound of breaking glass behind me. I knew big brother was in a lot of trouble.

So you can imagine my shock when Mom and Dad came home and Richard announced, "Ted broke the bookcase." This warping of the facts and bending of the truth was such an outrage! I defended myself saying, "*You* threw the shoe!" But he answered with what to this day he claims is ironclad logic, "But you ducked. It wouldn't have broken if you hadn't ducked!" Mom and Dad were not amused.

Adam and Eve tried the same tactic. After tasting the forbidden fruit and being questioned by God, Adam blamed Eve, and even God indirectly. "The woman whom you put here with me—she gave me fruit from the tree, and so I ate it" (Genesis 3:12). And Eve blamed the serpent when in actuality they had no one to blame but themselves. As the sad story ends, Adam and Eve have certainly fallen. They have fallen for a series of half-truths and lies. That is what makes temptation so, well—*tempting*.

"Did God really tell you not to eat from any of the trees in the garden?" Lie. "No. Only one tree. If we eat of the tree of knowledge of good and evil, we will die."

"You certainly will not die." Half true. They would not die immediately but would become subject to death because they would be denied access to immortality which they already had through the tree of life.

"Your eyes will be opened." True, but not in the way they expected. Now their eyes would be opened to a new experience, guilt and shame.

"You will be like gods, knowing good and evil." But they would know good and evil as human beings do, not as the Creator who knows what is best for his creatures. And they would make their own decisions.

Look around the world today. How is that working out for us? Sort of reminds me of parents of teenagers in that struggle about knowing what is best. I had a friend who used to tell his kids, "Until you are eighteen, *I* make all your mistakes."

The tree of the knowledge of good and evil is the tree of limits. It is the tree of "creatureliness." As Father John Kavanaugh once observed, Adam and Eve were good but they were not God. And that is what made them so vulnerable to temptation. Eat of this tree, they were told, and you will be self-sufficient, no longer dependent, no longer bound to God. One big massive lie.

The same subtle lies that worked so well in the garden of Eden, the Devil tried once again with Jesus in the desert. *You're the Son of God. You deserve to eat after all. Why not turn these stones into bread?* This is the lie of self-sufficiency all over again just like the next at*tempt* from the rooftop of the temple. *If you're the Son of God, make God rescue you. You can have all the power in the world if you give yourself to the Lie.*

But here the Devil met his match. Jesus refused to turn stone into bread for himself, but he would multiply bread for others and even turn bread into his body to feed the world. He refused to show off his power just to get attention, but he would consistently and humbly do the will of the Father. Jesus refused to grasp at worldly power, but instead he would wash the feet of his own disciples the night before he died.

Eden is restored in Gethsemane and the tree of the cross becomes the new tree of life. The Big Lie is defeated by the Naked Truth.

But so often naked truth is difficult to face, especially the truth about ourselves.

Every year the season of Lent presents us with the opportunity to face the simple truth of our own limits: our weaknesses, our selfishness, our mistakes, and our sins. The annual season of Lent can also be our chance to let God heal and restore what is broken in us. God does not leave us alone in the desert. Remember the last line of Matthew's gospel account of the temptations of Jesus in the desert: "and behold, angels came and ministered to him" (Matthew 4:11).

The First Mass

Luke 24:13–35

This well-known story in Luke's gospel might very well be considered an account of the first Mass offered after the resurrection. As such, the story offers a wealth of insight into what we do every time we gather for the celebration of the Eucharist. The following reflection on the story is intended to spur thought and deepen insight into the Mass. It is suggested that you read Luke's story as you follow these comments.

Two disciples on their way to Emmaus on Easter Sunday afternoon were walking along having an animated discussion, struggling to understand all that had happened, maybe even arguing over it. Events surrounding their hero, Jesus of Nazareth, had not gone the way they had expected. In fact, all the hopes and dreams they had placed in him had been dashed to pieces. Then Jesus joins them on their way, but they fail to recognize him. Were they distracted or depressed, or was this just too much to hope for? Did he look different? We don't know. Still, they were traveling in the company of Jesus without even realizing it. And as the story unfolds they were drawn to this "stranger," listening to him on their way.

How does this story have anything to do with our experience of going to Mass? Isn't it really what happens as we gather for the Eucharist every time? What were you thinking about when you arrived at church last Sunday? What was your conversation about? Were there problems to solve, schedules to establish, errands to run? Maybe even disagreements? When you walked into church did you realize Christ was already present as he promised he would be when two are gathered in his name? Did you do any better at recognizing him than the two disciples on the road to Emmaus?

Of course the Mass is far more structured than the Emmaus story, but essentially the same reality is happening. Mass begins with the introductory rites:

The entrance procession and hymn. It is then that we first speak with one mind and one voice, one unified song of praise. The ministers—servers,

122

lector, presider reverence the altar, symbol of Christ's presence with a bow. The presider reverences the altar with a kiss.

Greeting. "In the name of the Father" equals "in the presence of." We are gathered in the presence of the Father, the Son, and the Holy Spirit. We have come to Mass to open ourselves to God's presence whether we have actually recognized it or not at this point. Recalling we are in the divine presence we are now ready to reflect on our baptismal call to be salt of the earth and light of the world.

The penitential rite. It takes different forms, but they all call us to remember our own weakness—the salt has gone flat, or the light has gone dim or even out. But this is not to make us feel bad about ourselves. Nor is it meant to make us feel guilty or ashamed. The penitential rite is a reminder that we can sometimes forget that God is present in ourselves and in each other and that we can and have, on occasion, harmed others as well as ourselves.

The prodigal son had a similar realization when he returned to his father's loving embrace. That is where we are in the penitential rite—not judged, condemned, or punished but rather welcomed home to the Father's loving and forgiving embrace. Did you ever notice that in the story of the prodigal son the father never says "I forgive you"? He doesn't have to. Instead he orders a feast. The feast is the forgiveness just as the Eucharistic feast is our welcome home. Forgiveness has already been given. How often do we think of the Eucharist as a sacrament of forgiveness—yet it is, along with baptism, anointing of the sick and, of course, penance itself.

Father Timothy Radcliffe has said that when God forgives our sins he is not changing his mind about us, he is changing our minds about him! (Timothy Radcliffe, *Why Go to Church?* 18) With that experience of divine love, compassion, and forgiveness the community moves quite naturally to an expression of joy.

The Gloria. "Glory to God in the highest ..." Where have we heard these words before? At Christmas, when the angel of the Lord was joined by a "multitude of the heavenly host saying glory to God in the highest and peace on earth to those on whom his favor rests" (Luke 2:14). Whenever we sing the Gloria we echo the song the angels sang at Jesus's birth. Now we are ready to focus.

The opening prayer (sometimes called "the collect" because it is intended to collect us all together in prayer). This prayer is quite brief and to the point and usually mentions in a general way the theme of the Mass for the day. The introductory rites conclude with the opening prayer.

Liturgy of the Word. When we left the two disciples on the road to Emmaus they had just told Jesus his own story without having the slightest idea they were in the presence of the risen Lord himself, as we always are at the Eucharist. Now it is Jesus's turn to respond, and he sounds impatient at the very least, if not downright annoyed! "Oh, how foolish you are! How slow of heart to believe all that the prophets spoke! Was it not necessary that the Messiah should suffer these things and enter his glory?" Then, beginning with Moses and all the prophets, he interpreted to them what referred to him in all the Scriptures. They would soon respond, "Stay with us!"

What is happening here in this story parallels what happens at every Mass from the first reading through the general intercessions. We call this part of the Mass the liturgy of the Word. If this sounds like an exaggeration, the general instruction of the Roman Missal says, "When the sacred Scriptures are read in the church, God himself speaks to his people, and Christ, present in his own word, proclaims the gospel."

Something began to stir in those two disciples as they listened to Jesus along the way. We know this because when they came near their destination and Jesus indicated he was traveling on, they pressed him to stay with them. There was something about him that touched them, spoke to their hearts, and gave them hope. What words in the Scriptures have done that for you?

The liturgy of the Word has a structure that begins with:

The First Reading: usually taken from the Old Testament and always related in some way to the gospel that will follow. (During the Easter season this reading comes from the Acts of the Apostles, depicting the life of the very early church.) The first reading is followed by our response:

Psalm response, which in turn is followed by the

Second Reading: usually taken from one of Paul's letters but sometimes from another New Testament letter or book, like Revelation.

The second reading is followed by the *Alleluia Verse* sung as a fanfare for the gospel. We stand as a sign of respect for the gospel and Christ present in his word.

Gospel—Matthew, Mark, Luke (John in the Lenten and Easter Seasons) tell our story as a faith community rooted in the teachings, life, death, and resurrection of Jesus. Like the two disciples on the road to Emmaus, it is Christ speaking to us, whether we recognize him or not.

Now comes *the Homily*. It is said that when Caesar of Arles preached, the doors of the church were locked to keep people from fleeing. Fortunately for congregations today, there are safety and fire codes that do not allow the doors to be locked. The homily is an attempt to relate our lives today to the Scriptures. Much the way Jesus did as he explained the Scriptures and their meaning to his two disciples on the road to Emmaus.

The homily is followed by the *creed*. This is a very compressed expression of our faith, of what we believe in. Sometimes this is the very ancient Apostles' Creed and sometimes the Nicene Creed, which was composed in 325 CE at the Council of Nicea. It draws on the reflections of the early Christian community on its own experiences and expresses those reflections in the language of Greek philosophy which was how the world was understood at that time. That may help to explain why some words or phrases may seem puzzling or curious to you.

The liturgy of the Word comes to a close with the *general intercessions or prayer of the faithful:* having heard the Scriptures and reflected on them we turn our attention to the needs all around us in the world. This is where minds tend to wander, and we tend to respond almost mechanically without paying close attention. We shouldn't!

I had a classmate who used to threaten to insert his own prayer into the general intercessions that went something like this: "That all those not paying attention to these petitions be struck by lightning, we pray to the Lord ..." It was his way of highlighting that when we pray these petitions we need to realize we are not just asking God to "take care of" this or that particular concern as if God were our servant, or "divine genie." That would be incredibly arrogant. Rather, by raising these petitions to God we are actively committing ourselves to see that with God's help we may make them become reality. If we pray for peace, how are we going to further peace in the world? If we pray for compassion or justice, how are we going to make those happen in our own lives? If we pray for healing, we may not be able to bring physical healing to someone but we can bring our own concern for them and place them at the feet of the Lord. When we pray for healing for someone else we act like the four friends of the paralyzed man who lowered him down and placed him at Jesus's feet (Mark 2:1–12).

The general intercessions conclude with a simple prayer that leads into the liturgy of the Eucharist. We are now at the point where the two disciples invite Jesus, saying, "Stay with us."

The Liturgy of the Eucharist

We have seen Jesus join the two disciples on the road to Emmaus on Easter afternoon. They tell him his own story and then he responds by interpreting all the Scriptures that referred to him for them. As he speaks, we will later learn, their depression begins to lift and hope returns. This much of the story corresponds to our gathering in the presence of the Lord and then listening to his word at Mass. Now we rejoin them in the story for Luke's extremely brief but densely packed account of the Eucharist, they shared with the Risen Lord.

The two disciples invited Jesus to stay with them and "it happened," Luke tells us, "that while he was with them at table, he took bread, said the blessing, broke it, and gave it to them. With that their eyes were opened and they recognized him, but he vanished from their sight" (Luke 24:30–31). In these few words Luke describes what happens at Mass during what we now call the liturgy of the Eucharist.

As with the liturgy of the Word, the liturgy of the Eucharist is more structured than in the story, but the underlying reality is the same.

The liturgy of the Eucharist begins with *the preparation of the gifts*: the bread, wine and water brought forward at offertory time symbolize our lives. The paten bearing the bread comes through the community and as it does it collects the life of each person here—all our gifts, talents, accomplishments, hopes, plans as well as our fears, failures and anxieties. That paten should be pretty heavy by the time it reaches the altar. All our lives are raised up on that paten, offered to the Father and we ask God to transform them—to transform us. This happens several times. The first is when the water is mixed into the wine with the prayer, "By the mystery of this water and wine may we come to share in the divinity of Christ who humbled himself to share in our humanity."

The second comes as the presider extends his hands over the gifts during the Eucharistic prayer, again a plea for God to transform us. The preparation of the gifts concludes with the prayer over the gifts. Then comes a little dialogue: "The Lord be with you … it is right and just."

What follows is called the *preface,* which gets its name from the fact that we are now standing "before the face of God" as Isaiah did when he was called to be a prophet. Isaiah saw God seated on his throne surrounded by fiery angels called seraphim who called out to each other: "Holy, Holy, Holy is the Lord God of hosts" The temple shook to its foundations and the sanctuary was filled with smoke (Isaiah 6:1–4). This was an awesome experience. As with the Gloria, when we sing "Holy, Holy, Holy" we echo the song of angels and are reminded of the solemn holiness we are about to encounter.

But then we add the words of the psalmist: "Blessed is he who comes in the name of the Lord" (Psalm 118:26). The king was welcomed into Jerusalem with these words, as was Jesus on Palm Sunday, bringing salvation and the very presence of God in his person as he does at Mass. Following the preface comes the Eucharistic prayer. Altogether there are ten of these but the ones you are likely to hear most often are Eucharistic prayer II and Eucharistic prayer III. All are addressed to the Father through the Son and the Holy Spirit. All follow the same pattern.

"And so, Father, we bring you these gifts." Remember these gifts are our lives. "We ask you to make them holy …" It's not just the bread and wine we pray to be transformed, but ourselves.

Now comes the *consecration.* He took bread, gave you thanks, broke it, and gave it to his disciples … which is exactly what Luke tells us Jesus did for his two disciples. This is how Jesus told his disciples to remember him and this is why the two disciples suddenly recognized him. Up to this point they were *not* remembering him this way. All they saw was tragedy, pain, humiliation and failure. They had even told Jesus about the events earlier that day when some from their group went to the empty tomb, saw the stone rolled away and the burial cloths and then they concluded, "but him they did not see." John Shea points out, "When you remember Jesus as a reputation, a victim, a failure, and a dead man, 'him you will not see'" (Shea, *Gospel Light*, 172).

Now suddenly they recognize the Risen Lord in whose presence they have been all afternoon. In one more twist of irony, Luke says at that instant Jesus vanished from their sight. But as they looked into each other's eyes they now found him present.

Now they really saw him! Do we see him in each other? The Eucharistic prayer continues. We remember his passion, death, and resurrection—the "paschal mystery"—and we remember we are united to the entire church—those present, others around the world, those who have died.

Doxology literally means "giving glory." The presider holds in his hands in the consecrated bread and wine the Creator of the universe, and yet it is the Creator of the universe who holds him and the entire congregation in his hands. Truly a reason to give glory! We leave the two disciples now realizing their startling epiphany that Jesus is indeed risen. They are filled with excitement at their discovery and can hardly contain themselves.

Communion Rite and Dismissal

As the two disciples looked into each other's eyes they saw him present although they could no longer see him physically. Excited by this revelation they exclaimed to each other, "Were not our hearts burning within us as while he spoke to us on the way and opened the Scriptures to us?" They were so excited, Luke tells us that, "They set out at once and returned to Jerusalem where they found the eleven and others gathered with them" They could hardly wait to share the good news—what we now call the gospel.

This is actually what takes place at every Mass. And, as with the other parts of the Mass, once again this part is more structured than the story, But again, the underlying reality is still the same.

The Communion rite begins with the "Our Father." This is an extremely powerful and challenging prayer, but it is also terribly familiar, *maybe too familiar*. So familiar that we can easily fall into *reciting* it—and I use that term intentionally—without really considering its meaning. Jesus began by calling God "Our Father," but he certainly was not the first one to do so. The prophet

Malachi said, "Have we not all one father?" (Malachi 2:10), and Moses himself asked, "Is [God] not your father who created you?" (Deuteronomy 32:6).

So by saying "Our Father," we acknowledge we are daughters and sons of God, brothers and sisters of one another as well as brothers and sisters of Jesus himself. In fact, this is our deepest identity, kinship with God and Christ. Here we are already in the embrace of divinity and we haven't gone beyond the first two words. One could go on at great length reflecting on the power of this prayer, but for now maybe we just need to remember how the rest of the prayer expresses our dependence on God and, like the General Intercessions, challenges us to work with God in bringing about the Kingdom through unity, justice and forgiveness. In the words of Father Timothy Radcliffe perhaps the best way to sum up the Our Father is to say that it expresses our hunger for a "larger love."

The Our Father leads quite naturally into the *sign of peace*. The sign of peace is not just a casual greeting. It's not a "Hello. How are you?" It's a little late in the gathering for that kind of greeting. The sign of peace is the expression of our willingness to ask for and to give each other forgiveness. It comes just before we approach communion remembering Jesus's instruction: "if you bring your gift to the altar and there recall that your brother has anything against you, leave your gift there at the altar, go first and be reconciled with your brother and then come and offer your gift" (Matthew 5:23–24). We also remember the words we just prayed in the Our Father: "Forgive us as we forgive one another."

The sign of peace is followed by the *breaking of the bread*: the host is then broken into pieces to be shared by the community. It is through this action that the two disciples recognized Jesus, and it is through this action that we are to recognize him as well. The one bread and one cup remind us we are all one body of Christ. The Lamb of God recalls John the Baptist pointing out Jesus as the paschal lamb who gives his life for us and to us. "Lord, I am not worthy that you should enter under my roof but only say the word and my soul shall be healed" (Luke 7:1–8) recalls the faith of a pagan centurion.

Communion received with open empty hands. It is in this moment we become the Body of Christ, which is what we mean when we say "Amen."

Or as St. Augustine put it, "Receive what you are. Become what you receive." That's why we call it "Communion."

A silent period of reflection is now followed by the *prayer after Communion,* and then any announcements regarding the life of the community.

Mass concludes with the *final blessing and mission* The two disciples set out at once to share the good news. Now we are commissioned to go out into the world of our daily lives to do what they did: announce the good news, the gospel. That does not mean we need to be "preachy" but rather that we live in our everyday life what we have celebrated here.

Leon was an immigrant in the early twentieth century. He lived a very simple life and didn't have much, but he and his wife managed to raise a family during the Depression and always found reasons to give thanks to God.

One day a friend of his was complaining about the state of the world. Nothing was right; everything was wrong. It became a long, sad litany of woes.

Finally, Leon said to him, "Hey, do you believe in Jesus?"

"Yes," the man replied.

"And do you believe he died for you?"

"Yes."

"And do you believe he rose from the dead?"

"Yes."

Leon concluded, "So what are you worried about?"

Raised Up

Job 7:1–7; 1 Corinthians 9:16–23; Mark 1:29–39

When my brother, sister, and I were growing up, we spent many wonderful summers at Conesus Lake. The dock in front of our cottage was not terribly long because about twenty feet from shore there was a drop-off where the water grew very deep and you could no longer see the bottom. One afternoon, Cathy, the next door neighbor's six-year-old daughter, decided to take her little two-year-old brother, Greg, for a ride in their rowboat. Greg sat precariously on the seat in the very back of the boat while Cathy rowed happily about. But then, as she rowed near the end of our dock, she decided to pull particularly hard on the oars. The boat lurched forward, and little Greg flipped out of the boat and disappeared under the surface of the deep water.

Fortunately, our dad saw it happen and like a shot ran down the dock and dived into the water. Seconds later we saw Dad's two hands burst through the surface, holding aloft a coughing, startled, but otherwise safe little boy.

The Scriptures sometimes tell us that God holds us in his hands just like that no matter what kind of peril we may find ourselves in. Today Jesus literally takes the hand of Peter's mother-in-law and raises her up, delivering her from a life-threatening illness and restores her to health and life. In response, she immediately sets about waiting on her guests.

Now, right away it needs to be said here that this is not some kind of self-serving miracle. Jesus never performed miracles for his own personal benefit. Consider Jesus's temptations in the desert (Luke 4:1–13), his trial before Herod (Luke 23:8), and even his time on the cross (Luke 23:39). Still, some actually wonder about Jesus's motives here, as if he almost asked, "What do you have to do to get a sandwich around here?" Of course, that is not at all the sense of what is happening here.

Some Scripture scholars have pointed out that the fact that Peter's mother-in-law gets up immediately is a sign of how complete her restoration to health is, but Mark has other points to make here as well, and it all has to do with power.

When Jesus took Peter's mother-in-law by the hand, he "raised her up."

The word Mark uses here is the same word the angel uses on Easter morning to announce that Jesus "has been raised up" (Mark 16:6). This incident with Peter's mother-in-law is a foreshadowing of the resurrection. But it is more than that. Jesus did not perform this healing for his own personal benefit, and the new lease on life Peter's mother-in-law received was not just for her own sake alone. Her first impulse is, like Martha of Bethany, one of hospitality: serving the needs of others. It is no accident that Mark uses the word *serving*. It is the same word Jesus used when he told his disciples, "Whoever wishes to be first among you must be your servant, for the Son of Man did not come to be served but to serve" (Mark 10:44–45). The gift of life is given to be a gift of service for others.

Jesus would demonstrate that service in the dramatic scene that follows. That evening, after dark, the whole town gathered, bringing their sick and those possessed with evil spirits. Jesus moved out of the house and confronted the darkness outside. Illumined only by the flickering light of lamps and torches, he moved through the darkness of pain and suffering with compassion, healing, and life—his life, a gift given for others.

And there is the challenge of this gospel story. How are we of service to others? How do we follow in the footsteps of Jesus through the darkness of need, hunger, pain, loneliness, and suffering in our world to offer compassion, concern, and comfort? We may already be serving others with our gifts as caregivers, teachers, protectors, guardians, healers, or mentors and never thought of it that way. Who knew? But the crowd outside Peter's door was large, and the needs were many and great. Can we recognize them when they are right there before our eyes?

God has raised us up by the hand and commissioned us to a life of service to others. How are we doing?

The Easter Egg

Mark 16:1-7

Many years ago I gave a series of homilies to the youngsters and their families who were preparing for First Communion. Each week, they would attend a class before Mass and learn about a different aspect of the celebration of the Mass, the Eucharist. Each lesson had a particular theme, like "It's about Belonging," "It's about Caring," or "It's about Giving Thanks." One week the lesson was "It's about New Life," so that Sunday I brought in a large paper "seed" I had made. We talked about seeds and how you plant them and then flowers grow and how different the seed looks from the flower. Then I unfolded one of those brightly colored accordion-folded flowers to make the point.

Next I asked the boys and girls what kind of new life comes from eggs. Then I brought out a large papier-mâché egg I had made. What no one knew is that I had hidden a live baby duck in the egg. When we talked about what might pop out of this egg, I took my hand off the top and out popped the head of the duck peeping as loudly as it could. The children were out of their seats.

Weeks later, on First Communion Sunday, I was invited to the home of one of the children for a party. As things were getting underway, the hostess called me aside, saying, "I have to talk to you." Whenever I hear those words, I wonder what kind of trouble I'm in. Then she said to me, "Do you remember the Sunday you brought the duck to Mass?" Who could forget? Then she went on. "As we were leaving Mass that day, Annie looked at me with a deeply puzzled expression and said, 'Mom, I have a question about that duck.'" She said she panicked thinking this was going to be a serious conversation about life's beginnings and she was not prepared. So she did what any experienced parent would do. She stalled. She told her daughter, "Okay, Annie, when we get home and you change your clothes, we'll sit down and you can ask me your question about the duck."

All the way home she was agonizing about what to say, trying to decide how much to say, how to phrase things so her answers would be age appropriate. She was a nervous wreck wondering if she was really up to the task.

Well, when they got home and Annie had changed her clothes, mother and daughter sat down in the living room and Mom said, "Okay, Annie, what do you want to know about the duck?" Annie's brow once again got deeply furrowed, and then she said, "Was that a *Catholic* duck?"

The Eucharist *is* about new life. It is about eternal life. It's about resurrected life—not resuscitated life, not a return to the old life, but a new life that lies far beyond our present earthly experience and even beyond our wildest imagination. And that is why we resort to analogies just as Jesus did. Analogies and symbols like seeds that give birth to flowers or even apple trees, cocoons that break open to release butterflies, and of course eggs that burst open to produce baby chicks and ducks. In each case the life that each contains is only a hint of the life that will emerge.

And so it is with resurrection. On Easter morning the Risen Jesus had a life so vibrant, so powerful, and so dynamic that even the solid stone walls of the tomb could not contain him but cracked open like an eggshell. That same life is given to us in baptism and is nourished at the Eucharist. Eternal life is ours already because Jesus rose from the dead. *It's heaven in the orchard.*

Bibliography

Katz, Richard. *Sacred Stories: A Celebration of the Power of Stories to Transform and Heal*. San Francisco: HarperSanFrancisco, 1993.

Kavanaugh, John F. *The Word Embodied: Meditations of the Sunday Scriptures, Cycle A*. Maryknoll, NY: Orbis Books, 1998.

Keating, Thomas. *The Mystery of Christ: The Liturgy as Spiritual Experience*. Rockport, MA: Element Inc., 1991.

Lazarus, Emma. "The New Colossus," poem for the dedication of the Statue of Liberty, 1903.

Levine, Amy-Jill. *The Misunderstood Jew, the Church, and the Scandal of the Jewish Jesus*. San Francisco: Harper Collins, 2006.

McPherson, James M. *To the Best of My Ability: The American Presidents*. New York, NY: Dorling Kindersley, 2001, 367.

New American Bible. New York, NY: Catholic Book, 1970.

Radcliffe, Timothy, *Why Go to Church? The Drama of the Eucharist*. London: Continuum, 2008.

Remen, Rachel Naomi. *Kitchen Table Wisdom*. New York, NY: Riverhead Books, 1996.

Robinson, John A. T. *But That I Can't Believe*. Fontana, 1974.

Shea, John, *Gospel Light: Jesus Stories for Spiritual Consciousness*. New York, NY: Crossroad, 1998.

About the Author

Father Ted Auble currently serves as assisting priest at the parish of the Nativity of the Blessed Virgin Mary in the village of Brockport located in upstate New York. In addition to having ministered in several other parishes, his pastoral experience includes participation in the Rochester Interfaith Jail Ministry, college campus ministry and the Muslim Catholic Alliance, a group dedicated to promoting mutual understanding and cooperation between the two faith traditions.

Before ordination he taught English as a second language as a Peace Corps volunteer on Cheju Island in South Korea.

His previous book is entitled *Divine Sparks: Gospel Stories Discovered in Everyday Life.*